Digital Giving

Digital Giving

✦

How Technology is Changing Charity

Richard C. McPherson

iUniverse, Inc.
New York Lincoln Shanghai

Digital Giving
How Technology is Changing Charity

Copyright © 2007 by Richard C. McPherson

All rights reserved. No part of this book may be used or reproduced by any means, graphic, electronic, or mechanical, including photocopying, recording, taping or by any information storage retrieval system without the written permission of the publisher except in the case of brief quotations embodied in critical articles and reviews.

iUniverse books may be ordered through booksellers or by contacting:

iUniverse
2021 Pine Lake Road, Suite 100
Lincoln, NE 68512
www.iuniverse.com
1-800-Authors (1-800-288-4677)

Because of the dynamic nature of the Internet, any Web addresses or links contained in this book may have changed since publication and may no longer be valid.

The views expressed in this work are solely those of the author and do not necessarily reflect the views of the publisher, and the publisher hereby disclaims any responsibility for them.

ISBN: 978-0-595-44255-3 (pbk)
ISBN: 978-0-595-88586-2 (ebk)

Printed in the United States of America

Contents

Introduction
Technology Never Turns Back

Everyone knows one important thing about technology: it never turns back. If it makes life easier, more fun, cheaper, or richer, it's here to stay. Every day we see how new technologies are changing the ways people hear the news, connect, share stories, pursue interests, spend money, and sound off about their opinions. These are, of course, most of the activities that determine the success of nonprofit organizations competing for attention and support.

I embarked on a series of interviews, conducted expressly for this book, to get a broad perspective on what these tech changes mean to nonprofit organizations. The following chapters are based on those conversations which took place over about ten months and took me from Google's growing campus in California to a North Carolina schoolroom. I asked for input from technology companies, social observers, media experts, and some of the savviest people in what I'll call "charity." That's just shorthand for philanthropy, the voluntary sector, or whatever you prefer to call the million-plus U.S. nonprofit organizations that work for social justice, the environment, the arts, children, health, education, and the full range of causes Americans hold dear.

These individuals were exceptionally generous with their time and ideas when asked two questions: What are the big technology trends affecting charity, and how can organizations embrace them to increase public support? I wasn't asking for mere tips—though plenty were offered, and all are passed along in these pages. I wanted strategy, insights, and lessons learned, given with unvarnished candor. Interviewees were asked what surprised them about technology trends, what they found challenging or easy, and what advice they had to offer. As you'll see, everyone delivered heroically, each agreeing to serve as a virtual advisor to you and your cause.

You'll be relieved to know that I've used only a dozen technical words or acronyms, and only those because you will hear them frequently as they rapidly enter the vernacular. And, although there are many useful books that can enlighten you, I have only cited five, each listed in the resource section and each deserving your time. Some live on as Web sites worth a visit.

Let me stress that this book is not an uncritical love letter to technology, portraying a digital utopia in which the Internet and cell phones save struggling organizations. In fact, one lesson from the technology revolution is already clear—a bold vision and good management will always have more impact than technology. So will poor focus and bad management. Organizations that struggled before the iPod will do so long after it is replaced by the latest phone-camera-laptop combination. Groups that have always served their constituents well are positioned to use technology to ignite huge increases in public support.

I wrote this book because I believe enormous technological changes, daunting as they may seem to busy nonprofit organizations, will be for the better. Why? Because new technology is rapidly removing obstacles to participating in the causes we love—learning about needs, telling others, giving money, and seeing its impact. In that spirit, this book is dedicated to everyone who looks for new ways to connect people with a good cause.

1

Three Whopping Big Trends,
Ready or Not

You've sensed it for some time now, but have been too busy to sort it all out.

The Internet finally seems faster, and the search function is now second nature to you. You barely noticed when cell phones took over the world and vaguely wonder if reports of "e-mail addiction" just might be true. Writing a paper check makes you feel increasingly like a monk with a quill pen. And you're glad to have five hundred channels, but seem to watch less television.

You're off to a good start because you understand the big picture. More important, you're ready to spend a couple of hours doing something essential in the frenzied world of 24/7 demands: you're ready to pause and reflect. What do all the changes mean, especially to those who labor to help a good cause?

Whether you are an executive, manager, board member, or donor for a nonprofit organization, your charity's success increasingly depends on forces that are uncomfortably new. The press is overflowing with reports of technology changes roiling industries from entertainment and communications to retailing and politics. The stock market races to keep pace, not just with tech companies, but with their products' disruptive effect on everything else. These new forces are proving to be fundamental because they are social and cultural, which is why they will change charity as surely as every other enterprise.

To learn exactly how people are using new technology in ways that affect your favorite cause, let's first check in with the mother of all sources, the Pew Internet and American Life Project. And don't worry if the name sounds a bit academic—the data and conclusions are dynamite. Did *you* know the average American home has twenty-six electronic devices? Or that the average American spends more time using media than any other activity?

Let's see what else the project can tell us.

Media is now "as available as the air we breathe."
Advice from Lee Rainie, director of the Pew Internet and American Life Project

It's no wonder you feel constantly plugged in. About 30 percent of your day is spent *solely* using media—phone, TV, Internet, iPod, whatever. You spend an *additional* 39 percent with media while doing something else. How do we know this? Because of an organization led by a helpful fellow named Lee Rainie, who agreed to be your first advisor.

Lee was managing editor of *U.S. News and World Report* before he decided someone needed to track the impact of the Internet on Americans' lives. He founded and directs what most people just call "Pew Internet." From a nerve center in Washington, Lee's team measures how technology affects the way we live and communicate. Because it started in 1999, Pew Internet can do far more than map the obvious growth of online activity; it can reveal emerging trends that are literally reshaping how people communicate, find information, and meet their social and personal needs.

Clearly the biggest change of all is the ubiquitous nature of media, present in more than two-thirds of our waking day and resulting in what some observers are even calling media dependence. Whether we are dependent or not, we are surrounded by media that is increasingly shaped by our own preferences. The consequences are important to charities:

- People need more help sorting out the relentless information flow and are turning to technology to make "rapid judgments on what's useful, using their own horse sense," according to Lee.

- People now expect to find information and to find people whenever they feel like it with a click or two. This means they go online to find a useful group—or they'll simply start one themselves using the cheap, easy tools of what's now called social media.

- These social media technologies have enabled Americans to become their own publishers and media producers. Pew Internet reports that one-third of Internet users either produce a blog or journal, post photos or comments, or create their own Web pages (including those to raise funds for their favorite charities). Like all other do-it-yourself media, this number is growing rapidly as the tools become more familiar.

"Here's the big thing we see," Lee says. "As information becomes super-abundant, people become more dependent on help to sort it all out and validate the information. That means depending on referrals (from friends and trusted sources) and social networks."

So are people becoming more distrustful of experts and authority? Not exactly, according to Pew data, which shows that one in five Internet users have signed up to receive alerts from news or other "authoritative" organizations. Credentials still mean a lot, which is good news to the charities that Americans use to help them understand humanity's needs.

But expert advice notwithstanding, people depend increasingly on other Internet users (their peers) to "prioritize and rank information and content." Twenty-eight percent of all users have tagged or rated something, from blogs and news stories to photos and even charity projects, according to Pew Internet, and the number is increasing. And about half use online bulletin boards, listservs, and similar sources to stay up-to-date on topics of interest to them.

Lee stressed that something else is occurring that is worth noting: "As people gain experience online—and as the experience becomes ever more useful—people become more serious in the things they do online." Americans report to Pew that the Internet "played a crucial or important role" during what Lee Rainie calls "major life moments," such as choosing a school (45 percent), dealing with a major illness (26 percent), or finding a new job or place to live (33 percent). This has boosted people's willingness to make financial transactions online, something that 71 percent of all Internet users report doing.

There is an abundance of great information at Pew Internet's Web site, which is included in the indispensable resources section at the end of this book. But let's move on with our journey and look into three trends that are changing charitable giving in ways that will be permanent.

Trend #1: The democratizing of media

To traditional media producers, this trend is very painful and feels more like doom than democratization. As you will see in chapter three, Americans now spend less and less time getting information from the daily paper, the evening news, or even AOL, which already finds itself categorized with mainstream media. Cheap, easy technology tools have produced the explosion of "citizen journalism," quantified by Pew Internet. More and more, people are getting their information from blogs, podcasts, viral campaigns to tell-a-friend, personal Web pages, and social networks with names that make it impossible to mistake them for mainstream media: MySpace, YouTube, Friendster, Flickr, Care2, Gather, Squidoo, and many more.

This trend means that people, not editors, are deciding what constitutes the news. And it means that people, not media, are deciding what issues and organizations will receive attention.

It's worth emphasizing that I don't mean to glorify decentralized, grassroots communications by using the word democratization. Democracy often isn't pretty. Blogs are producing countless dedicated citizen journalists willing to tell truth to power. But social media also allow others to rant with little regard for the truth or civility.

In the final analysis, the quality of citizen media improves, like democracy itself, when more people participate actively with widely agreed-on rules and with a genuine stake in the process. We'll look at the issues and lessons surrounding this trend, discussed by your advisors from organizations both large and small.

Trend #2: The democratizing of philanthropy

Blame it on the culture of the Internet for making donors choosy, outspoken, and impatient. Or celebrate it for speeding dollars to worthy but obscure projects. However you view this trend, it's a whopper, because it means the donors are taking over from the fund-raisers when it comes to deciding what gets funded. It is nothing less than the radical democratization of philanthropy.

People who contribute money expect a say in exactly (and I mean *exactly*) how their money is used. They expect plenty of choices. They expect feedback on the results. And they expect it promptly, on their terms.

Just like electoral democracy, philanthropic democracy at its best will be responsive, enjoy broad participation, and be rooted in the best values of the community. At its worst, it will at times be chaotic, polarizing, and subject to manipulation.

Whether you are pleased or worried by this trend, the truth is technology provides donors with a bigger voice in decisions that used to belong to managers of charities. Nonprofit organizations have historically served as filters, deciding which funding priorities saw the light of day; they will now have to add the role of advisor and advocate, presenting programs whose fate will increasingly be decided by a marketplace of donors armed with the ability to find information fast and compare notes with others.

The result will be greater pressure on traditional charities to be more accountable to the public and their donors, and to provide the kind of responsive relationship previously reserved for those able to write big checks.

This trend, moreover, is producing another outcome that is starting to catch the attention of Americans: the rise of an entirely new kind of charity, previously impossible without twenty-first-century technology. We'll look at four examples with different objectives but with two things in common: First, none even existed more than three or four years ago. Second, they all have a growth curve that is virtually unprecedented in philanthropy, going literally from zero to millions of dollars raised, often in a matter of months.

And don't think for a minute the pinstripe crowd can avoid donors' demands to have a voice in charity decisions. We'll see just how this trend is already beginning to affect the way major corporations relate to charities and even how they allocate their philanthropic dollars.

Trend #3: The relentless demand for convenience

You're thinking, "I paid fifteen bucks for this book, and he's telling me the secret is just making it easy to donate?" Believe me, it could be the best advice you'll get today.

According to our friends at Pew Internet, "new technologies have enabled us to become a culture of multitaskers." One-fifth of you are on the phone while online, another fifth are online while watching television, and almost half of you read the newspaper while watching television. I saw no data on how many of you send text messages while barreling down the highway with your Starbucks balanced precariously, but I'm sure the number is terrifying.

Think about it: if you've ever felt stuck in a process that was a waste of your time, you probably put it off until later or skipped it altogether. The plain truth is that charity—giving away money—is probably not a task considered essential for most people on most days. As important as charity is, it must compete with the thousand personal demands, distractions, and pleasures that make up our lives. Far too often, giving money away is just not that convenient.

Of course, the concept of making it easy to donate has been with us for years in the form of nonprofit "affinity" credit cards, Paul Newman's salad dressing, and bar-coded disaster relief donation coupons at supermarkets. Even state governments are in the act, offering checkboxes allowing tax filers to support everything from senior citizens to wildlife preservation. But while these donation methods are well-intentioned and fit conveniently into people's lifestyle, most have two big downsides: they usually result in small transactions, sometimes only pennies, and more important, they provide little or no personal connection between the donor and the charity.

Technology is now offering greater convenience plus two-way communication between donors and organizations. You'll see how a ballet collects contributions using an ATM. You'll find out what's going on with cell phones and charity. And you'll learn how supporters can and do raise millions for their favorite charities—*if* the tools are easy to use.

You might sum up these three trends with one observation: as the competition for donations intensifies, successful charities will be the ones that offer the most engaging variety of donation choices, endorsed and promoted by friends and peers, with the most convenient paths to involvement.

Let's turn this information into practice. Just switch off your electronics and turn the page. It's time to demystify all that cool new technology and meet your next advisor.

2

Succeeding on "Web 2.0"—Whatever the Heck That Is

It's the buzz phrase that attempts to capture the new world of online social networks and do-it-yourself tools that give increasingly greater control of the Internet to users at the expense of institutions.

It's "Web 2.0," and if you can't define it, don't fret. Technology leaders don't even agree on the name. World Wide Web inventor and alpha-guru Tim Berners-Lee harrumphed recently that "nobody even knows what [Web 2.0] means." But the prevailing feeling was expressed by Sheeraz Haji, founder of GetActive Software, acquired by Convio in 2007 and where he is now president. He admitted to me cheerfully in a recent interview, "I have drunk the Kool-Aid of Web 2.0. It's a fundamental and radical change in the way people communicate."

Observers and experts largely agree. Whatever you call it, the latest stage of the technology revolution means one thing for sure—don't get too comfortable with your existing Web site or your carefully crafted e-mail strategy.

Darn it. Just when you were getting the hang of updating Web pages and segmenting your e-mail list, along comes a whole new Web to think about.

Not to worry. In just a few pages, you'll be as savvy as the next person, able to nod wisely in any meeting and take advantage of trends that can mean new support for your cause.

Keep in mind that the point of all these new online tools is to advance technology pioneers' dream of a more democratic medium, free from the influence of people like you, me, and "The Man," who sit in offices and try to control the Internet. It's worth remembering that in 1990 when Mr. Berners-Lee invented the technology allowing anyone to publish, share, and find information among the world's computers, he refused to patent his invention. He wanted everyone to participate without needing anyone's permission. That spirit drove—and still drives—the Internet's evolution.

Here's what all the fuss is about and why it's so important to your organization:

The "old" Internet you know so well is readable. The new one is also writeable.

The old Internet was virtually owned by institutions that were able to create Web sites and organize content. The new one is owned by users who are able to create and organize content themselves.

You may feel like all this crept up on you; no one threw a switch and shut off the old Internet, replacing it with a new one. There is still plenty of old stuff online. But though Web 2.0 changes are evolutionary, it is a very fast evolution.

To understand how the Internet is changing, and how your organization's approach must change as well, think of Web 2.0 broadly in two ways—as a social impulse and as the technology tools that enable it.

- As a virtual social movement, the values of Web 2.0 include open communication without filtering by authority, information that is more accessible because it is organized by users, and do-it-yourself content in almost any form. Oh, yes, plus the ability to share and reuse content freely. Web 2.0 is growing directly from the original intent of the World Wide Web's developers.

- Technologically, Web 2.0 describes a wide range of online software applications that allow people to create, change, and share content freely in almost any form. Words, pictures, sound—you name it. Familiar examples include blogs, personal Web pages, and discussion areas. This "many-to-many" and "few-to-few" publishing is often called social software because it enables people to connect easily with like-minded souls. Web 2.0 applications also include "group editing" sites called wikis, which allow any Internet user to edit a Web page, resulting in a kind of collective wisdom. Popular online encyclopedia Wikipedia, by the way, offers a fascinating explanation of Web 2.0, and the Web site itself demonstrates effective group editing, complete with differing points of view.

All well and good, you say. But group editing? Many-to-many publishing?

If this highly democratic social media sounds tough to control and a bit chaotic, then you already understand a major challenge of the new Internet. These are often called the Wild West days for Web 2.0. But just as the sheriff, the schoolhouse, and indoor plumbing all came to Dodge City, some rules and lessons are emerging as the Web changes. In fact, one development is positively comforting: the new online tools neatly fit the culture and needs of nonprofit organizations.

"Finally, nonprofits have the advantage."
Advice from Sheeraz Haji, president of Convio

Early online developments were dominated by commerce; somebody had to put up the money to get the Web where it is. Retailers taught us how to shop online, travel sites taught us how to compare prices, Napster's Shawn Fanning and Apple's Steve Jobs taught us to download songs, and banks taught us about passwords and paying bills. But according to Sheeraz Haji, "Nonprofits should actually dominate Web 2.0 because it's all about passion and interest. And the low cost of many online tools, especially compared to traditional media, answers the challenge facing many organizations—a small budget."

Is Web 2.0 affecting e-mail, which is cheap and used heavily by charities? Without a doubt, says Sheeraz: "The days when it was fun to get e-mail are long since over, and e-mail is often ignored by younger people. The key is helping people use their own words and pictures to communicate with friends and family. After all, they are the core of our life experience." Thus the rapid rise of MySpace, et al., and the importance of personal, not institutional, e-mail.

As a technology provider to hundreds of nonprofit organizations, Sheeraz and his Convio colleagues quickly learned "how incredibly big and powerful advocacy is, how badly people wanted to get involved." The one-way nature of twentieth-century mass communications left behind, in effect, a huge, pent-up demand to be heard. "The Internet made it possible," Sheeraz adds, noting that even groups with no political or policy agenda benefit from giving people the chance to share their enthusiasm, whether it is for art, children, healthy living, or good books. For a while, people enjoyed the novelty of being involved online; now they expect it.

For his last piece of advice, Sheeraz chose not to talk about technology at all: "To get people involved, your organization has to tell a great story." Focus on the message before worrying about delivery channels, and remember the Internet rewards inspiration: "Be completely brilliant."

Whether your organization is a leader online or just wants to get more out of technology, it's useful to look at those who are trying almost everything the new Web 2.0 has to offer. That certainly describes the ASPCA, whose ambitious program is shepherded by Jo Sullivan, your next advisor.

"You can't go into this ready to be defensive."
Advice from Jo Sullivan, senior vice president for development and communications, ASPCA

Online, people are getting used to speaking up and sounding off—sometimes loudly. This explains the popularity of the booming online social networks (see chapter five). Your supporters will speak up on your behalf and will do so in their own words. "These sites are fun and interactive," said Jo during our interview, "but you can't go into this ready to be defensive. People will say what's on their mind."

Of course, Jo Sullivan is careful, as your organization should be, to become involved in established social networks that place a premium on civil dialog and monitoring. ASPCA favorites are MySpace, You-Tube, Care2, and Squidoo. If any of these are unfamiliar, better get online and spend an hour or two; they are the meeting places for active donors and volunteers. But, much like a public meeting or even your own orchestrated events, you can't control every word of the conversation.

This democratization of communications applies not only to content but to the frequency of contact with your organization. It's a tough shift for organizations accustomed to setting schedules for newsletters, annual reports, and so on. Online, people expect to decide for themselves how much e-mail is too much. They increasingly expect to pick the topics and frequency of e-mail you send them, or they will use the most effective tool at their command—the delete button. They may not drop their online subscriptions to your e-stuff, hedging against the day when your subject line may seem relevant to them. Industry-wide tracking studies are reporting a nationwide epidemic of steep declines in e-mail open rates, plus a dive in the number of people willing to click back to a Web site, which strongly suggests that content driven solely by organizations is fast losing importance to recipients.

The ASPCA works hard to provide a flow of e-communications that is heavy on customization, offering state and federal legislative alerts, blog invitations, links to YouTube videos, cell phone text alerts (see chapter nine), and multiple e-newsletters based on interests and pet preferences. All of these choices are highly automated, demonstrating that only user-managed technology, not human labor, can meet the increasingly high expectations of picky Web site visitors and e-subscribers.

Are these new do-it-yourself donor tools raising more money for the cause or just moving it around? When the ASPCA initiates an appeal from its development operation using almost any medium, Jo observes, contributions are largely from their base. "But when it's viral [appeals initiated by supporters], it's new money," she says. Give supporters the communication tools, a clear charitable need, and a good nudge, and you're playing by the new Web 2.0 rules. In other words, the megaphone effect of engaged online supporters applies to advocates and volunteers as well as donors.

Does this mean everyday users want to become columnists, reporters, and personal editors on the new Web? Exactly. Let's see how the word "media" is getting an entirely new meaning—and what it means to your organization.

3

Citizen Journalism—Did Someone Just Change the Channel?

America's defining phrase has changed from "We the People" to "We the Media," according to the title of an important book by Dan Gillmor, who founded the Center for Citizen Media. As a veteran newspaperman for some of America's leading dailies, Gillmor's new career resulted from his epiphany that his readers had become his collaborators. As he quotes Jeff Jarvis of Advance Publications, "The Internet is the first medium owned by the audience." To charities, that means it is owned by the donors.

Thanks to Web 2.0, the audience is flexing its muscle with the growing popularity of new tools, including little things that seem to spring from the ground overnight—blogs.

How the virtual world provides a dose of reality.

There are an estimated sixty million blogs, and more new ones are added daily. With so many editorial voices, some blogs are inevitably drivel and thankfully languish unnoticed. But a great many are drawing wide participation, focusing on issues and reaching people important to charity. The "blogosphere" is one of many technology phenomena that can help meet an important need of charity, which is to reach targeted groups of people inexpensively and credibly. The last point is especially important: the most wildly popular blogs are the products of motivated individuals, not marketing departments.

In their book *Citizen Marketers: When People Are the Message*, Ben McConnell and Jackie Huba hit the nail on the head: "The most successful work in this new world of media comes from a place of authenticity, not calculated deception or stealth marketing … Social media is the antidote to campaign-based thinking."

Blogs, they point out, "may not be a quantifiable feedback system, but [they do] create a front-row seat for companies interested in real-time opinions." Or, they might have added, for charities interested in being at the center of developing public opinion rather than on its margins.

The authenticity of citizen journalism is the reason that blogs have proven powerful enough to sink the plans of political candidates, force the resignations of prominent religious and media figures, and dramatically alter the strategies of major corporations. They are certainly powerful enough to rally support for an important cause—if used wisely.

Of course, encouraging supporters to speak up for your charity online is a step fraught with anxiety for nonprofit organizations accustomed to guarding their message carefully. Your virtual advisors have some thoughts on this very point; just as you provide a press release or media interview and must play by certain rules to receive coverage, you will need to learn the ways of participating in new citizen media.

First, let's talk briefly about three little letters that will be very important to you: RSS.

Really simple stuff.

RSS usually means Really Simple Syndication, or sometimes Rich Site Summary, both describing its function: RSS allows people to subscribe to receive only the information they want from blogs or Web sites, and the feeds are sent directly to their computer or other preferred device. There's no need to trudge through Web sites, clicking away for information or repeating searches. RSS is your personal Internet organizer, and according to Gillmor, "could well become the next mainstream method of distributing, collecting and receiving information."

RSS is forcing mainstream media to tolerate the use of their content in bits and pieces. For example, you may not want an entire magazine online but can receive an RSS feed of only the topics you do want. Quoting technology expert Chris Pirillo, Gillmor sums up the power of RSS: it "suddenly makes the Internet work the way it should. Instead of searching for everything, the Internet comes to you on your terms."

Just think about how your charity uses mainstream media to reach people, and you'll see the potential in citizen journalism, such as blogs, and the use of RSS. Nonprofit organizations can rarely afford to buy media space. More often, they become media beggars, pleading for coverage through press releases, events, occasional op-ed articles, or the attention offered by a celebrity endorsement. Often, the media attention so painstakingly earned is swept away in the very next news cycle. And of course, earning "free publicity," as any public information officer will tell you, is anything but free, requiring time, talent, and expenses.

Now, online social media offer an alternative that has three big benefits: it can be more effective, it's cheaper, and "coverage" of your issue does not vanish as long as people want to keep talking about it.

If traditional media is fragmenting, how do you get attention?

Nonprofits basically face a simple choice when communicating online: attempt to aggregate people to learn about their cause, or go to aggregators who have gathered a virtual crowd for them. Clearly, the latter is more effective for reaching a broad audience.

Although the world of blogs is often thought of as a sea of opinionated individuals, Pew Internet's Lee Rainie observed that "many bloggers now think of themselves as aggregators, posting lots of links to what they believe are the most reliable or useful sources." A key step for a growth-minded charity is to search for bloggers who serve this purpose for their cause, and then contribute to the discussion and be part of the link traffic.

Okay, we know RSS helps you be your own virtual channel, programmed by your supporters to stay in touch with you. And blogs can be your free media strategy, keeping the conversation going. How about using somebody else's "channel," especially if they have lots of the right kind of people? Let's get some insights from an online destination that's being called "MySpace for grown-ups."

"Half our members are older than 42, and they post a comment every 3 seconds." *Advice from Tom Gerace, CEO of Gather.com*

Compared to MySpace and its millions of members, Gather.com is small, boasting only a few hundred thousand members. Only? My, how the magnitude of the Internet has made us casual about numbers that are remarkable to database-dependent charities.

Although many describe it as an online community, Gather's motto emphasizes that communication is its mission: "Media of, by and for the people." With more than two hundred thousand people contributing content to more than 7,200 interest groups on Gather, its claim is entirely legitimate.

When Tom Gerace talks about Gather and other social media groups, he stresses that their importance is rooted in providing members with publishing tools. "Our Marconi," he told me during our interview, "was the software that allows ubiquitous, free publishing tools. It used to cost hundreds of thousands of dollars to create and publish video or music. Only a few big companies could afford it. Now it's free, and it's changing the way people communicate entirely."

Is he exaggerating?

Not if you consider that more than sixty million people in the United States have already published something online, from modest blogs and podcasts to films and photo journals.

"It's a giant leap for knowledge sharing," Tom insists. "People share what's on their mind with friends, family, and colleagues, who are all just a couple of clicks away." What's more, "the information is relevant, trusted and social." In a statistic that supports Tom's view dramatically, he points out that "MySpace now has two or three times more traffic than *The New York Times*, CNN, or even AOL. And people spend up to ten times more time on content created by individuals than content created by traditional media."

Okay, I'm impressed. What can we learn about succeeding with social media? Tom has a few pointers:

- **People will check you out.** Gather has five unique visitors for every one member on its site. (Do you know the ratio of visitors to members for your Web site?) So be sure to have a wide variety of ways to get involved. Simply offering your e-news won't cut it.

- **Test paid search advertising.** Gather regularly buys ads on Google to build membership, purchasing, for example, the names of all U.S. Senate and House candidates in the last election. People searching for information on any candidate anywhere were offered a link to Gather's "Politics" discussion area. People clicked, and membership boomed. (We'll visit Google in the next chapter.)

- **Monitor but don't interfere in community discussions.** Worried about people getting carried away? "We were surprised that people wanted to do more than just publish their opinions," Tom says. "They want to help manage and edit. That creates a lot of social pressure to keep the debate civil and useful."

- **Natural leaders will appear.** Look to your online community members who make themselves heard and are respected by other members. Contact them, encourage them, listen to them.

Just in case you're thinking that online communities are the playpens of the young, I asked Tom about some of the most active groups on Gather. "I would include 'Living at its Best,' set up for AARP members." These Gather members are the "mature" and aging constituency of AARP; they discuss travel, health, the environment, and many other topics. And they are opening plenty of eyes to the growing influence of seniors online.

Tom added that a healthy social media site will attract much bigger, mainstream media players who need a place for focused discussion. "Amazon created a Gather group for writers to discuss and learn about publishing contracts," he said. Simon and Schuster conducted a "First Chapter Contest" on Gather, where aspiring writers submitted the beginning of their book, the online community picked finalists to create a second chapter, and so on. The writers write, the community rates, a new book is born.

Of course, Gather was established to be both a new media channel and a social community. How would a traditional, issue-based non-profit organization use technology to find and recruit donors?

Let's look at two examples, one an established billion-dollar charity and the other a boot-strap start-up. The first group crafted multiple, virtual channels from divergent partners, while the other is turning an army of small donors into a citizen-journalist channel.

Bringing "odd actors together" with spectacular results.
Advice from Katherine Miller, Director of Communications, the United Nations Foundation

A billion-dollar pledge from Ted Turner could have made a lesser organization complacent or at least could have stifled innovation. Not for the people at the UN Foundation.

After all, who would expect the UN's American supporters to connect with *Sports Illustrated* and the National Basketball Association (NBA)? Yet they did exactly that in order to mount a dramatic and effective online campaign to fight malaria in 2007.

It's a story of mobilizing tens of thousands of new donors in a remarkably short time—all made possible with technology and a willingness to look beyond traditional channels to spread the word.

Like many good stories, it began with one person who had what I would call a charitable epiphany, in this case Rick Reilly, a highly regarded columnist for *Sports Illustrated*.

"$10 can actually save a life? It's a no-brainer," Rick said in an online article for *Sports Illustrated* that started it all. He noted that sports fans talk about nets, games with nets, all kinds of nets. But he had no idea that a simple anti-mosquito bed net could prevent malaria and actually save a life. And it costs only $10 to buy and deliver one to Africa.

Rick decided to use his popular online column to tell people about the nets and tell them to get moving and contribute. The UN Foundation created a "Nothing But Nets" (NBN) campaign, complete with its own Web site.

The concept rested not only on reaching many people online through a new media partner but also on tapping into a growing online fundraising phenomenon—encouraging small groups to form teams online and raise money on its behalf. Launched before the beginning of 2007, the NBN campaign quickly had 264 "teams" across the United States raising money online in a matter of weeks—almost a tenth of them affiliated with local NBA teams to increase the reach in local communities.

Notice how the strategy was launched and expanded in cyberspace but drew on local loyalties. One can easily imagine thank-you activities at packed professional basketball games, generating still more contributions and affording a high-energy thank-you for donors.

How did it work?

Within weeks of the launch, NBN raised $1.3 million and generated twenty thousand e-mail addresses from new supporters. In the next few weeks—just the time it took me to write this chapter—the campaign hit $4 million.

The project is a textbook case for using new technology to communicate: The UN Foundation created a new, virtual, and probably even temporary "channel": they borrowed *Sports Illustrated's* reach online, used NBA teams as local megaphones, and pulled it together with a project-specific Web site used by groups of online volunteers to raise money.

What's next for the UN Foundation as it explores technology for charity?

Saving world heritage sites around the globe, the magnificent but fragile, threatened places people love to visit.

And what is the channel strategy this time?

Create a partnership with Expedia, the online megasite for travel. Promote responsible tourism, draw attention to a need, and make it fun with a contest. In Katherine Miller's words, echoed throughout my interviews, "Go where the people are."

"Trust is most important."

Asked to give my readers the benefits of her experience, Katherine named four lessons:

- **Third-party validation is important.** Online, you should be prepared to reach a lot of people who may not know you or who may not think of you as a place to donate. Associations with Google, the NBA, Expedia, AOL Black Voices, and others were key to earning the trust the foundation needed with new audiences.

- **Don't get sucked into the tech movement of the moment.** Develop a comprehensive strategy using new as well as old media. While online promotion generated 70 percent of NBN contributions, 30 percent came by check in good old-fashioned envelopes.

- **Technology is just another word for grassroots.** Think first and foremost about where your potential supporters are, how they get information, what motivates them, and how to make it easy to be involved. Then pick the technology and the partners that fit.

- **Keep your message and campaigns simple.** Katherine added extra emphasis to this point, commenting, "We fought to remind our partners—and ourselves—of this." The UN Foundation was tempted to explain their institutional impact and plans. They settled for one donation, ten bucks, one net. The temptation is to treat your newfound audience to the grandeur of your mission, the breathtaking genius of your programs, and … well, just don't do it. A first date is not the time to start discussing china patterns.

What if you don't have a billion-dollar backer like Ted Turner? In fact, what if your total media budget is closer to zip?

A spunky start-up with "zero budget" shows how to be your own channel.
Advice from Kiva Communications Director Fiona Ramsey

Microfinancing may not be charity in the traditional sense, but it sure packs a wallop fighting poverty, because a little money can go a long way in the right hands. Microfinancing is the process of loaning tiny amounts of money to men and women in developing countries to help them become self-sufficient by starting a business.

The concept has been around for some time; what's changed is the advent of an entirely new kind of nonprofit organization, existing purely because of technology that brings budding entrepreneurs and "lenders" together online, usually across international borders.

There's no better example than Kiva.org. One of Kiva's striking features, besides its skillful use of technology, is the role you are offered after you decide to participate—spokesperson for the organization. I'll walk you through the process, which is an eye-opening lesson in how to equip your supporters to become an active, independent communication channel.

I went to Kiva's site and looked at dozens of projects, listed catalog-style, and chose to help Victor Burgos. He plans to expand his tiny Ecuadorian clothing store to sell small kitchen appliances. A local development agency provides business training for Victor, whose store in the small city of Guayaquil supports him and his three children. Thanks to Kiva, by the time I came across Victor, he had gathered all but $50 of the $1,050 he needed to expand. A couple of mouse clicks later and I was an international financier, putting the last $50 in the pot.

The terms of my loan were spelled out: Victor expects to pay me back within six to ten months through a simple deposit into my PayPal account. I can then take my money back or reloan it to another business. I'm not worried—95 percent of all loans are repaid.

There's another confidence-builder: 100 percent of my loan goes to Victor because Kiva, like many of the new charities (see chapter six), makes its overhead an optional contribution. Kiva offered me a choice: "Help Pay the Rent" or "Skip this step." At 10 percent overhead, I gave the extra tax-deductible $5, convinced by the straightforward explanation and photos of Kiva's staff in their modest office.

Feeling rather pleased with the experience so far, I moved on to "Get Involved with Kiva," a Web area that is a virtual tutorial in using supporters to spread the word. Besides the usual request to e-mail my friends and colleagues, I was encouraged to:

- Put a banner on my social network profile, blog, or Web site (with plenty of cut-and-paste examples provided)

- Join Kiva's YahooGroup to see how other people and businesses are helping in local communities

- Go to MySpace, Friendster, Squidoo, and FatWallet, all of which feature a "kivaloans" section

- Be a Kiva editor or translator to help polish the proposals sent by ThirdWorld working poor to Americans (and then tell my friends what I did)

- Write a blog or post a comment on an existing one
- Create art about Kiva (sorry, this book will have to do)
- Send Kiva my own ideas on how to spread the word, guaranteeing that supporters will generate their own strategies for attracting their peers

Activities like e-mailing friends will likely appeal to the older lender-donor, while participating in social networks probably will attract a younger set, at least for now. The point is that there is something for everyone, and the strategy is leading to a multigenerational support base for Kiva, something traditional charities often struggle to achieve.

Kiva's Fiona Ramsey reminded me that traditional media continues to play a big role in raising awareness of the organization. But with what Fiona calls a "zero budget" for conventional public relations and marketing, Kiva must focus on building its own grassroots communication channels.

Kiva's leaders knew they had to take advantage of online social networks as a communication channel because those channels can be accessed without payment and because Kiva's donors itch for things to do. Kiva requested from YouTube some visibility on its highly prized Web site. Its request granted, the YouTube channel now delivers one out of every ten visitors to Kiva's Web site.

Kiva also asked its lenders, whose loans average $70, to start their own Yahoo Groups to help draw attention to the organization. Hundreds signed up, and now there are fund-raising activities in dozens of local communities, providing a virtual chapter network.

Last, but far from least, all that e-mail forwarding, art making, blogging, and so on produces a steady flow of messages to potential backers from Kiva's supporters. It's cheap and highly effective, tapping the deep desire for unfiltered authenticity that comes with grassroots communication.

About a month after my loan-donation, I received an update by e-mail from Victor. It was written by him in Spanish, as Kiva explained in English, to save him (and them) the cost of translation. My Spanish is rusty, but that was no problem—Kiva provided a handy link to an automated, online translation service. I could click, get a translation, and feel much closer to Victor, Kiva, and the impact of my gift. It actually made me feel a very real part of an international organization; for a few minutes, I was visiting my project with Victor.

You're probably wondering what this citizen-powered channel has actually produced for Kiva.

In a growth curve that would humble philanthropic veterans, Kiva recruited thirty-five thousand people to loan and donate a total of $3 million—just in its first ten months. And would you care to guess how many lenders add the optional contribution for Kiva's overhead? A quarter? Half? In fact, more than 85 percent do so, helping guarantee that this new player will stick around.

Actually, Toto, we *are* in Kansas.

The words "museum" and "history" connote old stuff. But museums have become good places to learn how to develop your own channel and create content that is easily shared by individuals. Their podcasts allow visitors to hear erudite commentary without waiting in line to rent a clunky, outdated device the size of a prison brick. What's more, you can listen at your leisure before, during, or after your visit. Many museums use their podcasts to boost membership contributions; when you visit, just show the device you used to download your tour and join at a discount.

Now that cell phones are merging with iPods and other portable recording devices, it's easier than ever to download audio and take it with you. The sky's the limit for enterprising organizations that want to murmur their latest news in donors' ears or take them to visit a project no matter how far away. In an early hint of the potential of this technology, UNICEF experimented with offering podcasts from areas affected by the devastating tsunami. They were stunned when the podcasts were downloaded three million times—in a day long before iPods were everywhere.

Do we need to go to such a huge organization or to a metropolitan museum with a megabudget to see a good example? Actually, all we have to do is visit Kansas.

The Kansas State Historical Society Web site at www.kshs.org offers "Cool Things Podcast" in which curators discuss particularly intriguing items in the museum's collection. Mindful that a channel has lots of competition for attention, they offer appealing podcasts on items including "Custer's Dumbbell" (he loved to work out and apparently went to Little Big Horn in great shape) and "Mickey Mouse Undies," a portrait of culture and family life in the Great Depression. In the "Kansas Memory" section, you can download readings of "Wanted" posters for runaway slaves or an invitation to dance at the Territory Social, complete with period music, naturally.

None of these audio offerings are promoted as discussions, gallery talks, or other stuffy-sounding monikers, but are simply called by the term any good channel would use: they are "episodes."

If you don't happen to have your iPod with you or didn't download a tour, some museums can fix that: the San Francisco Museum of Art can provide you with an iPod with its "artcast" tours already loaded.

Finally, some examples remind us that "mobile" need not mean just audio. Paris-based technology company Espro is retooling handheld game devices, turning them into touch-screen audio-video tours, allowing the hearing-impaired to enjoy tours in sign language at the Guggenheim Museum in Bilbao, Spain, and London's Victoria & Albert Museum.

When public broadcasting becomes "public media."

Hundreds of public television and radio stations serve every American city, town, and rural area. Many people will say, however, that if there is a "spiritual center" for public broadcasting, it is Boston. The nation knows WGBH as the leading producer of noncommercial programs, ranging from science and drama to investigative documentaries.

What many people outside of New England may forget—but what WGBH management can never forget for a second—is that the station is also a regional nonprofit organization depending on tens of thousands of dues-paying members for its existence. So the challenges of new communication technology and citizen journalism weigh as heavily on WGBH as they do on you, and they have given the subject plenty of thought. Your next advisor bridges the communication and nonprofit sectors in a unique way.

"My worry is that serendipity will go away." *Advice from Jon Abbott, president of WGBH*

"The opinion of a friend matters," Jon observed in our interview. "Blogs, podcasts, and social networks allow people to amplify their self-expression." But there's a problem on the receiving end: "People don't want all the noise that comes with such abundant communications," so they focus on sorting out what they want to hear. The problem is that "sorting out" means "shutting out."

"I think it's important, as you produce content, to offer people some kind of sampling function," Jon adds. "Some of our most popular and valued programs include those that people have simply stumbled across. This serendipity adds richness and excitement to media," including in Jon's view, the increasingly self-managed media of blogs and social networks. So while you give supporters the means to pick and choose specific content, don't be afraid to sprinkle your communication with the chance to explore a new topic or viewpoint.

Your charity, presumably an authority on its issue, confronts another question faced by WGBH and PBS: what is the relationship between authoritative content and citizen journalism?

Jon believes the process begins, first and foremost, with an organization providing "an online experience that is thoroughly credible." That means "being very clear about what your brand stands for and how you are distinct from other organizations." Provide dependable, accurate content that will start and inform discussions, recognizing that people will take up the conversation on their own.

Jon's example was the popular investigative program *Frontline*. The program, he points out, remains faithful to its mission and standards. What changes is that "there will be many new forums alongside *Frontline*, bringing a greater diversity of voices to the discussion. It won't be just the elites having a voice, but a much more economically and culturally diverse group."

Despite decades of investment in television, radio, and Internet technology, WGBH is moving swiftly to understand and embrace mobile technology. "It is getting much easier for people to share what they care about," Jon says, "and mobile information has to be part of our thinking." Offering a profoundly simple strategy for using new technology, Jon says that public broadcasting must "follow the rhythms of our consumers."

Of course, most people know how to go online and find their public broadcasting station, PBS or NPR. But what about people who are looking for information about *your* issue or organization? How easy is it for them to find you, and have you considered "search" as a channel worth its own attention?

4

It's Not a Search, It's a Quest—Why Google Is a Verb

It was pretty obvious from the dawn of the Internet that our brains would soon be swamped by information overload unless someone could organize it. With the Web adding countless new pages every day, plus a bazillion blogs, YouTube videos, and social network activities, it's easy to see why search is as important to people as e-mail. Pew Internet reports that 91 percent of all Internet users send e-mail—and 91 percent use search.

Nonprofits are discovering what advertisers have already learned: To attract attention in a big way, don't go looking for people. Help them find you while they're looking.

Search engine optimization (SEO) rapidly emerged as a marketing specialty aimed at helping Web site owners tweak their pages with words, links, and clues that entice the relentless, robotic search process to give them a higher "ranking."

But why tweak, wait, and hope for the best when you can simply buy a short ad, pay a few cents per click, and appear right on the screens of people looking for information? Thus, the Google Adwords service was born, allowing anyone or any organization with a few bucks to be part of the endless flow of searches. (The minimum is a paltry $30 a month.) The concept worked so well that Adwords helped propel the company from a tiny start-up to one of the priciest shares on the New York Stock Exchange.

The point isn't that two smart guys named Sergey and Larry made billions. It's that Google and the other search engines have produced an entirely new virtual channel, constantly reprogrammed by users to fit their needs.

Visiting the Googleplex.
No kidding. That's what they call it.

Arriving at Google's complex in Mountain View, California, it's hard to believe this company didn't exist ten years ago. The employees clearly strive to preserve the original casual, democratic culture, despite the sudden need for street maps to explain their proliferating buildings. But after you get past the signs for employee massage rooms, exercise balls, and legendary lava lamps (I counted six almost immediately), you quickly realize that Google is very focused on its work and its role in helping people sort out the Internet.

A tiny clue is their entertaining practice of projecting search phrases on the reception-area wall in a slow, almost stately scroll. They are randomly selected, I was told, "not in real time and not in the U.S.," though they are overwhelming in English. Talking with Google employees, from executives to receptionists, you come to understand these wildly assorted groups of words may be mere curiosities to you and me, but to Google they are a real-time map of our collective conscience.

Wow. Too far out?

Not at all, in the minds of many social observers. Google is, in a very real way, cataloging what the world is thinking at any point in time, what people want, and, many say, what people plan to do next. They have a sound point: why would you search for information about something you didn't plan to pursue, a place you didn't plan to visit, or a product you didn't plan to buy?

If you want a glimpse at how people are tracking your issue and what they are finding, go to the Google Trends section of their Web site and "see what the world is searching for." Enter search phrases that capture your issue, and you'll instantly see a chart showing three years of search patterns, with any spikes identified with the news coverage that caused them.

While search certainly catalogs the public's fleeting fascination with a celebrity marriage, politician's gaffe, or consumer fad, it also records the steady flow of deeper human needs, people literally on a search. You can see it in search phrases that are starkly revealing for their brevity: "breast cancer," "global warming," "teaching jobs in Chicago," "adoption placement," and countless more.

Think about your own experience: Sometimes you search merely for a quick piece of information, but other times, your search is the beginning of a much longer, more important process. You are trying to get to the bottom of something, often to make a more informed decision about life, work—or charity.

Speaking of charity, a national survey recently showed that almost half of all Americans visit the Web site of a charity before deciding to give. And how do they find a charity? Beyond simply guessing your URL, which many do, search is the most popular method of locating a nonprofit organization online.

These searches represent constantly gathering groups of people that can be a charity's dream—large groups of people actually looking for information, many of them potential supporters on a virtual quest. As some nonprofits are learning, search is emerging as a vital and productive source for attracting new supporters—a "donor acquisition channel" capable of rivaling direct mail, broadcast, and other traditional media. Some of the case studies you'll see later integrate search as an important tool, especially when a charity's issue is in the public eye or when a charity is mounting a coordinated campaign around an issue.

"I could raise $5 million before four o"clock."
Advice from Sheryl Sandberg, vice president of Google

Sheryl has a pretty good vantage point for tracking both the power of technology and the needs of charity. She is vice president of global online operations and sales at Google and also a board member of Google's foundation and the Ad Council.

Visiting with her, it was easy to see the mix of enthusiasm and frustration that results from understanding both the power and limits of technology. Though she was quick to deny there is anything as monolithic as a "Google view" of the nonprofit sector, Google's relationship with charity was crystal clear: strive to put the most powerful tools possible in the hands of responsible organizations. After that, the organizations are challenged to make the most of the opportunity for wider exposure. Google's recommendation is to provide a link to a page on your Web site that specifically responds to the needs of the person searching, whether it is for information or involvement. Taking searchers to your home page and leaving them to figure out what to do next is not productive.

Certainly taking advantage of the search function can draw enormous attention to your charity and capitalize on the awareness of your issue that an important news story generates. But Sheryl Sandberg was very animated about hit-and-run fundraising (my phrase, not hers).

"It's twelve noon," she said during our interview. "I could go online right now and raise $5 million—before four o'clock—to feed children in Africa. But that wouldn't help if children were dying from drinking polluted well water. It wouldn't help solve the systemic problem of poverty and public health. Giving has to be a continuing effort to change things."

Search is a huge opportunity to attract the attention of thousands of people new to your charity, but it should be regarded as an opportunity to draw people into a process of learning about your organization, how you fit into their personal quest, and why they should connect with you.

Typically, this means using your few seconds of search fame to invite a specific action. You might provide a link from a search ad to a blog, podcast, petition, survey, or e-card. Whatever your first step, it should meet the searcher's need for help and meet your need to inspire the searcher to stay in touch with your charity. And it should be easy; people searching online do not expect wasted steps.

Moreover, when you buy search ads, you can make the process and expense more productive for your charity by narrowing your message to attract the type of new supporter you want. Want to teach people to understand child abuse? Test something like "learn the five clues to spotting child abuse." Want to change policy? Try something like "sign this petition demanding stiffer penalties for child abusers." Want donors to help provide direct assistance? "Sponsor counseling and shelter for an abused child." The more specific your call to action, the more quickly people will filter themselves into interested or not interested categories.

If you feel adventuresome, visit Google Labs, a part of the site that may not even be known to many charities. There you will see a range of "ideas that aren't quite ready for prime time," on which Google encourages feedback, criticism, and improvements. When I checked in recently, there were experiments that seemed mundane but useful: "Ride Finder" lets you locate the real-time position of your taxi or shuttle, sent to your handheld. Others were exotic, offering "detailed maps of Mars." But lab ideas in development also included new ways to provide search capabilities for the visually impaired and a new process for providing visitors to your Web site with summaries of useful links. New experiments are constantly popping up (it's where the popular Google Maps and Google Video started), and it would be great if more charity tech folks would drop in to see what's coming and to push Google to develop services useful to our sector.

When I asked Sheryl if nonprofits were taking advantage of Google Labs or contributing ideas for products, she seemed surprised by the question. "The whole process is based completely on protecting the privacy and anonymity of Lab users so they can be totally honest. We don't ask or know the source of feedback. We just test its usefulness." She added her hope that charities will use Google Labs to propose and help test new Google services.

In the end, Sheryl's advice to charities mirrored Google's guiding principle: when developing technology, focus relentlessly on the needs of the user (that is, your supporters), and the rest will follow.

5

Democracy, Social Networks, and the Demand To Be Heard

Your organization is probably already listed on MySpace, the alpha site among social networks. After all, MySpace listed almost sixteen thousand nonprofit organizations—and that was several weeks ago. There are no doubt more by now. This is all taking some getting used to by the tradition-minded philanthropic community.

Only a few years ago, the very words "online community" suggested questionable dating sites, product fanatics, or wonk-dominated chatrooms, empty as often as not. Today, the situation could not be more different. In fact, thanks to the explosion of free, easy-to-use tools for individual publishing, communities are becoming an incubator for serious political debates, social action—and charity.

The social network stats are by now are almost numbing to charities used to battling for incremental growth: 100 million-plus MySpace accounts (and climbing), video-centric YouTube sold for $1.65 billion to Google, Facebook's 16 million members (and climbing), flickr and its millions of photo-sharing enthusiasts, and scores of other social sites. Some emphasize their international focus—like LiveJournal, which has 12 million accounts, only about one-third in the United States—anticipating the rise of border-free charity.

Internet veterans like Amazon have long since moved beyond merely filling a retail need and have taken on many qualities of a community, providing a useful place to study the process. What began as a handy "rate-it-yourself" function for book-buyers has evolved into a thriving community connecting readers with favorite authors, offering podcasts, interviews by comedian-commentator Bill Maher, and, by the way, a section called Amazon Giving, which features its Nonprofit Innovation Award. Amazon's evolution is a forceful reminder of the increasingly blurred lines between doing good and buying good stuff and of the potential power of partnerships between charities and retailers.

Online networks for social action and engagement, of course, compete not for retail sales but for the affections of people willing to speak up or at least listen to others with a cause. These rapidly changing communities try to outdo each other by offering ever-easier ways for people to find those who share interests, have discussions either passionate or mundane, and frankly just experiment with new technology toys.

In truth, all the fuss about social networks comes down to one thing, expressed so well by your next technology advisor, Randy Paynter.

"The more connected people feel, the more active they'll be." *Advice from Randy Paynter, founder of Care2*

Randy Paynter should know. He started Care2 (short for Care 2 Make a Difference) just a few years ago as an online destination for conservation-minded people to connect, do good deeds, and buy green products. When I started this book, Care2 had about 5 million members. Ten months later, it topped 7 million, arrayed in scores of groups that leap into action when asked—petitions, tell-a-friend, events both real and virtual—whatever will help the scores of nonprofits appearing on their Web pages.

Care2 has become an invaluable model and laboratory for nonprofit organizations seeking to understand best principles for attracting, motivating, and keeping large numbers of advocates and donors.

I asked Randy if anything in Care2's rapid growth surprised him, and his answer is an important lesson:

"We were surprised at how disempowered people feel." Care2 touched a deep nerve when it offered a wide menu of involvement options. "We helped people discover there are actually a lot of things they can do to make a difference, and some are really easy."

Notice that Randy didn't say mind boggling or death defying. He just said easy.

It's a point too often overlooked by nonprofits: why does it have to be hard to lend a helping hand? Of course, issues like global warming, fair trade, and human rights are complicated, and fixing them is not easy.

Care2's response? Give people someplace to start. Something tangible that can be done today. Something they can proudly (and easily) share with friends and family.

Nonprofits began to hire Care2, a for-profit company, to provide online campaigns to recruit people willing to take action and give money.

The response has been remarkable and highly instructive. Nonprofits as large as Amnesty International and Defenders of Wildlife, and as small as a local PBS station, use Care2 as a virtual channel for reaching new supporters.

People may come to Care2 with only a modest curiosity, but, Randy notes, "Once people get involved, even on something like a discussion board, they do far more than ever." This isn't just talk. Data show that after their first couple of online activities, Care2's members' engagement increases exponentially, sometimes leading to dozens of new actions on behalf of favorite charities.

How can you succeed in a big way?
The secret is "superusers."

Forget the old rule that says 20 percent of the people provide 80 percent of the action. The key to a successful online community lies in what Care2 calls "superusers."

"It's more like 2 percent providing 98 percent of community leadership," Randy says. "The unwritten law of online social networks is that a few people contribute a huge amount of the value." They post comments, write thought-provoking positions, take the lead on petitions and e-cards, and generally keep beating the tribal drums for their community.

Every successful community, online or off, has its superusers. The key, according to Randy, is to "harness them by providing the tools they need." And this, he reminds us, takes some real thought. "It's a balancing act," Randy says, "giving the superusers the whiz-bang features they want while realizing that most people won't use them."

Think of physical world analogies. From nonprofits' annual meetings to local zoning commission hearings, the most active members of any healthy group need a way to be heard. The process encourages and shapes debates, and gives the participants a big stake in getting others involved. It's the same online. Simply putting up an e-card or survey won't do it if you want to foster real activity and growth.

What are the commandments for online communities?

Randy offers four:

- **Start with a clear idea of what you want your community to do.** Do you want your community to affect a public policy, become the leading place to learn about an issue, pressure the media, promote new artists, or take some other action? Just wanting people to be involved with your organization is not enough.

- **Plan for your superusers.** Provide them plenty of tools for producing content and activity. Let them experiment, and be willing to drop any activities that don't attract interest, even if you love them dearly.

- **Have a growth plan.** What's the point of getting a few dozen people excited? Aim for hundreds, thousands. Besides, any healthy community thrives on growth for validation and fresh energy.

- **Balance listening and leading.** Communities can get carried away or distracted by a few outspoken members, so provide direction and focus with a flow of interesting, useful engagement activities that support your mission.

Care2 has found one thing harder than it originally thought, according to Randy.

"E-commerce has been tougher than we thought," he said. "We believe there is power in affinity relationships between nonprofits and retailers, but it's really hard to make it pay." People understand the power of purchasing as a social action, and Care2 hopes online issue activism will affect consumer decisions, to buy a hybrid, for example, rather than an SUV. But for the moment, at least, online social networks seem more effective as a place to discuss purchases than to make them.

I asked Randy if he was skeptical of any new technology. He answered that "Mobile [handheld devices] may look more promising than it is" because of the risk that high traffic will result in lower participation.

Perhaps, but I'm inclined to disagree. There is growing evidence that the shift to handheld devices promises to be massive, probably the dominant technology trend of the coming years. We'll spend some time on this question in chapter eight, but for now, let's spend a few minutes with a woman with no time to waste—she's a mom.

Never argue with a mother—certainly not thousands of them. —The wisdom of MomsRising.org

Online film clips, nationwide house parties, shared "mommy stories," and a tough petition campaign demanding progress on issues from fair wages to children's health care. It's a pretty ambitious set of activities for a group that, as we go to press, is about one year old. How's that for using technology to hit the ground running?

MomsRising was founded on Mother's Day 2006 by Kristin Rowe-Finkbeiner and Joan Blades, perhaps better known for co-founding MoveOn.org. When Kristin and Joan advise others based on their start-up experience, they sound much more like veterans. Here are a few tidbits that Kristin offered to a conference of nonprofit media leaders:

- **Commit to experimentation, not to planning.** Try a variety of online engagement activities and stick with the ones that work—until they stop working.

- **Provide regular, concise communications.** MomsRising sends out a once-a-week e-mail focusing relentlessly on one idea. Too much information becomes wallpaper in the in-box.

- **Commit to educating your online visitors, whether they are members or not**. It not only adds depth and richness to the discussion of your issue, but also helps win others to your issue. After all, that's the whole point.

I would add to Kristin's list one of the most important strategic lessons for online engagement: don't go it alone. Visit MomsRising.org, click on its list of "allied organizations," and you'll find organizations ranging from think tanks and health-care coalitions to women's groups and unions. It's likely that the relationship of these groups with MomsRising varies, and for some, may simply consist of providing direct access to their constituents. But that, as we all know, is like money in the bank.

If your organization's list of "allied" organizations is equally extensive and your links equally varied, then you are right there with MomsRising as an online leader. If not, then you have room for plenty of growth.

Living in a new landscape.

Social trends unleashed by the wave of new technology are no more good or bad than those set loose by Gutenberg, Marconi, or Alexander Graham Bell. They simply are a fact of life. They also create a new set of rules for communicating if you hope to move people to donate, volunteer, or take up your cause.

We've focused on only two online social networks, and you might be thinking that I could have looked at many others, both larger and smaller. That's precisely my point. This new technology-driven trend is shaping up as a dominant force in online communications for social action, politics, and its cousin, charity.

What can you expect from this upheaval on a practical level?

- In terms of producing results (money, advocacy, volunteers), communication among social network members will, within a couple of short years, eclipse carefully scripted e-mail from institutions.

- Recruitment of volunteers through online social networks will become the largest single source for volunteer time in America.

- Charitable success online will be driven not by the size of your e-mail list or even your donor base, but by the number of people who are talking about you through social media.

While social networks are a huge trend, it's unclear whether charitable support will be drummed up through the meganetworks like MySpace or by smaller, more focused networks. Why? Because the obvious popularity of social networks will doubtlessly prompt some nonprofits to start their own. That is already getting easier, as *New York Times* correspondent Brad Stone reported in early 2007. Social networks, he wrote in an article scanning the phenomenon, are "sprouting on the Internet like wild mushrooms," and their popularity has prompted the rapid growth of companies that build custom social network sites or sell turnkey network-building software. Examples include People

Aggregator and Ning, whose founder Marc Andreeson believes that "existing social networks are fantastic, but they put users in a straight-jacket," according to Stone's article.

Stone also reported that many technology leaders see MySpace, Facebook, and the other biggies as "walled-off destinations, similar to first-generation online services like AOL, CompuServe and Prodigy," destined to fade because their millions of people have "ultimately, little in common."

So the experimenting has begun and you can expect the rise and fall of social networks to dominate Internet news in the coming years. Political candidates (always useful to watch for trends in tech innovation), the University of North Carolina, and the Portland Trailblazers have all jumped into the custom network game, along with newcomers like Shelfari, a Seattle-based network for booklovers that was interesting enough to draw an investment from Amazon.com.

What's the useful lesson for us?

Simply that Web 2.0 tools have unleashed a process for gathering and sharing opinions online that people find fascinating and fun, and that charities neglect at their peril. Would you like a list of three social networks on which you should focus? Sorry, it doesn't exist. Would you like good advice on how to respond? That I can do:

First, if you aren't a member already, join a social network or two that personally interest you or that you hear a lot about or that you just read about here. Take part, have fun, see what people are doing. It may be among the most stimulating and useful hours of your week.

Second, check around your organization, inside and out, and see where others are spending time online. Check your charitable competitors' Web sites and see what links and social media tools they are providing. (If they are involved with any of the online communities or networks, then you'd best join in; if they are not, then grab your chance to be a leader for your cause.)

Third, keep a close eye on the e-newsletters from major technology providers, especially those that serve the nonprofit sector. When there are major developments in social networking, you'll find them here first, often with an evaluation or case study. The more people in your organization—staff and volunteers—who read these industry e-newsletters, the faster you'll move up the learning curve, and the more practical ideas your charity will have.

The new social communities, and those that will surely pop up in the next year or two, are not only a growing force for traditional charities. They are also contributing to another megatrend that is starting to attract notice among donors—the rise of an entirely different kind of organization, based online, driven purely by donor choices, and determined to take charity to a new level.

Let's take a look and see what we can learn.

6

Here Come the New Charities

There is an ironic challenge faced by major charities: their huge budgets. Years of success have translated into budgets that run into the hundreds of millions, and despite a steady flow of successes, donors of modest means must wonder whether their few dollars would have a bigger impact somewhere else. They yearn for specific accomplishments, deeds done with their dollars.

In the age of citizen journalism and intense 24/7 scrutiny, it isn't enough to say that you slay dragons—donors now expect you to produce the body. The need to give donors a way to translate a huge budget into do-able deeds is at work when Habitat for Humanity tells you the cost of a box of nails or when the Heifer Project offers to provide an African family a goat for your contribution. The challenge of making giving tangible goes back two generations to the famous CARE package.

But new technology goes much further than providing examples. It actually puts the decision of how to use their gifts in the hands of donors, not nonprofit administrators. The result is not only changing donors' behavior, but also increasing accountability among recipients. The idea of a "donor marketplace" that literally selects some projects and rejects others was once the province of major donors and foundations; now hundreds of thousands of donors have a voice, thanks to technology. And they are using it.

Some people may raise the question of whether the democratization will help or hurt charity. Will widespread donor involvement in funding decisions make charity less effective because it is less "informed" by experts? Or will democratization be more effective because it draws on grassroots support and educates donors more effectively than broad appeals?

The debate over marketplace decision making is the subject of James Surowiecki's *The Wisdom of Crowds*, a seminal work that explores decisions made with broad participation. It is a book well worth your time to understand how, fundamentally, new technology can and will disrupt the traditional funding and fund-raising process. In fact, the first case we'll explore is a group that literally tested the concept by asking tens of thousands of donors to rate projects online—while asking a panel of programmatic experts to do the same. In 75 percent of all cases, the experts and the donors picked the same projects. One is left to debate whether the donors or the experts made better choices for the last 25 percent, but the lesson was plain: technology is making possible a whole new kind of nonprofit organization that marches to the beat of a very nontraditional drummer.

Two World Bank executives who worried about the inefficiency of getting American charitable money to remote countries wondered if technology could provide a solution. They believed it could, so they did what you or I would do—if only we had their nerve. They quit their jobs. They proceeded to start an organization, and along the way, sparked a powerful movement that is already reshaping American philanthropy.

Organizations can never have enough money—but projects can.

Advice from Dennis Whittle, founder of GlobalGiving.com

"I was a reasonably successful, non-risk-taking bureaucrat," said Dennis Whittle at the beginning of our interview, describing how he decided to co-found GlobalGiving with World Bank colleague Mari Kuraishi in 2002.

Why were Dennis and Mari so confident that the concept on donor-driven fund-raising would attract wide support?

"It's because of the confluence of technology and media," Dennis explained, which allows "coverage of results, not just problems." People will still see images of troubled areas of the world, but they can now connect directly with teams on the ground that are providing solutions.

GlobalGiving began with a pledge to "build an efficient, open, thriving marketplace" for connecting people who want to help solve problems with people who had solutions. Working with established charities to identify reputable projects in developing nations, Dennis and Mari organized them into eight areas from health and environment to education and technology. A customer-friendly Web site was developed along the lines of a catalog in which donors could shop for a specific project to help.

Initially, many projects were often virtual castoffs of major charities, valuable but unable to compete with other, bigger funding priorities. To some established international organizations, "GlobalGiving was a kind of outlet store," according to Dennis. That changed quickly as aid organizations realized the new group was adding to the value chain in several ways, thanks to its use of technology.

In many ways, the process is a donor's dream:

- Project budgets are shown to potential donors in single, straightforward Web pages with short project descriptions written "on the ground" by the people who will do the work, not by GlobalGiving. The exact amount of money needed—and so far raised—is detailed, along with the current status of the work.

- When a project hits its fund-raising goal, donors are told it no longer needs funding. But, using technology familiar to any Amazon book buyer, donors are directed to very similar projects that still need support. ("If you want to help educate girls in Africa, you'll be interested in ...")

- Donors can see exactly who the project managers are, and even e-mail them. Though very few do, the access and accountability are important.

- Technology, of course, works in both directions. Projects are required to report to donors every three or four months, unfiltered by GlobalGiving, language problems and all. The gift may be "virtual," but a personal message from a project leader in Afghanistan couldn't be more real.

Will this put a dent in contributions to big, traditional charities?

Dennis was emphatic: "We intend to unleash more giving. Our goal is to compete with consumption spending, not other philanthropic giving. We want to provide an experience that is so good, it feels better to give than to buy a new iPod."

GlobalGiving is advancing this goal by reminding people, "You could feed a village from your desktop," followed with a very public promise to "insure that 85–90 percent of your donation gets to local project leaders within 60 days." That probably accounts for their 400 percent growth rate—going from $3 million to $5 million in the twelve months before this book was published according to the organization's public material.

Dennis has straightforward advice to your organization as you ask people to support you online: "Give up being a filter. I know it's scary, but people expect to give and get feedback on their donations."

Speaking of feedback, it's worth adding that like most new, Web-based charities, the finances of GlobalGiving are aggressively transparent. Precious space on the home page of GlobalGiving.com provides links to two years' of financials and its IRS 990 form—something a well-known charity may not want or need to do. Because reading an IRS 990 is only slightly more fun than reading a soup label, I don't know how many people make the attempt. Leaving aside the fact that a 990 isn't nearly as revealing as many think, the point made by Global-Giving is clear: it has no secrets from its donors. It's an important message for people pondering a gift—and for other charities who aren't as transparent.

There could hardly be a more direct impact of technology-driven democratization on charity than thousands of donors collectively deciding precisely where millions of dollars will go. It is a trend that will surely put pressure on traditional charities to adopt more donor-driven project selection.

Of course, not all new charities have business models that look like GlobalGiving, which is seeking to establish a new brand and build a big base. What if someone simply wanted to bypass institution-building and use technology to raise money quickly and cheaply?

How to spend $60,000 and raise $1 million.
Advice from Ken Deutsch, founder of Direct Change

For large, traditional organizations, "online fundraising may not necessarily be a fundamental change," Ken said at the very beginning of our interview. "It may only add another tool. But new organizations like ours are pure creations of new technology."

The strategy of Direct Change.org is simplicity itself according to Ken: "We're turning supporters into fundraisers and eliminating a huge expense. Our goal is to bring new money to the table, not just move it around."

Why is that a big deal to donors, especially to international relief?

"The traditional process of how people donate to Africa, and how money gets there, is horrendous," Ken asserted. "With overhead, bureaucracy, and the rest, donors are lucky if a fraction of their money actually gets there."

Direct Change's strategy? Skip the institution-building process altogether and instead, after carefully selecting effective local African charities:

- Identify a tiny core—perhaps only 2 percent—of highly motivated American donors

- Turn them loose with the latest technology to do the fund-raising themselves, essentially to *be* the organization

"My entire setup cost, from charitable registration fees to technology and salaries, was less than $60,000." Ken's original goal? One million dollars in direct support for a range of African children's charities. If he makes it, Direct Change will surely qualify as one of America's most effective international charities—and it didn't even exist before 2006.

How does Direct Change plan to succeed? Not by gathering thousands of donors, but by drawing the attention of a highly targeted segment of activists—emigrants from Africa, Americans who have adopted African children, and Peace Corps alumni, for example.

"We're creating a volunteer army in the U.S.," Ken says. "They may be among traditional donors to international causes, but they will raise new money from people who are not." New people, new money. The charitable pie gets bigger.

The early evidence is that Ken's new group may well exceed its dream of $1 million. How?

By embracing another megatrend we're tracking—relying not on mainstream media but on grassroots promotion. In this case, the hook was a movie.

Entitled *God Grew Tired of Us*, the movie is no big-budget Hollywood extravaganza; it depicts what have become known as "the lost boys of Sudan." It has sparked an effort to build a much-needed clinic in the southern part of that country.

A partnership was struck with John Dau, one of three individuals featured in the film, who agreed to participate in Direct Change's efforts to raise funds. Screenings of *God Grew Tired of Us* across the United States began to draw attention to Darfur and to Direct Change. The movie Web site, in fact, offered a prominent link to Direct Change, once again illustrating how even a temporary arrangement can create an ad hoc channel to acquire supporters.

Taking matters into their own hands.

Ken Deutsch admits his surprise at the extent to which people used the Web site as a kind of incubator for their own ideas about helping. His experience is also a useful reminder that giving people the tools to help on their own also gives them a kind of permission to act on their own.

"We weren't prepared for how many people wanted to raise money offline," like the group of donors in Los Angeles who decided to have a fund-raiser for Direct Change. They persuaded a local hotel to donate space, showed John Dau's movie, charged admission, and sent in a "group" contribution.

And when did Direct Change learn of the Los Angeles event?

"We found out when we got their press release," Ken admits with a mix of chagrin and pride.

He remarked on the rapid growth of events planned by students using new technology: A Los Angeles high school donated the proceeds from its battle of the bands (almost $9,000). Another student used Facebook to gather 150 students to raise money for Direct Change. The Glasgow Middle School in Fairfax County, Virginia, conducted a "read-a-thon" to support Direct Change and set up collection boxes to capture offline student donors.

"Grassroots fund-raising works best," Ken said, "when the ideas are not mine, but come from people. That's why we have to be flexible in our strategy." He reported that New Mexico students recruited a local gallery to hold an art sale for Direct Change, and then set up a laptop to take credit cards for purchases using the organization's secure site. "No consultant would ever have come up with that idea," Ken says. Technology is merely enabling thousands of people who have the zeal and ideas for helping. Ken summed up the process in four words: "People create, we replicate."

When charity becomes tough love.

Reporting—what professional fund-raisers call stewardship—is deeply ingrained in the culture at Direct Change. Monthly reports are offered to all donors, which Ken admits is a challenge because small African charities must do the reporting. But it's the price of being featured on the organization's Web site and e-mail.

The feedback from African projects to American donors will never be mistaken for the detailed reports required by large, U.S.-based foundations. "They are mostly informal narratives, more like a blog or e-mail," says Ken. They are highly personal and timely, providing an intimate connection between people who help and people who are helped. I suspect these gritty updates will engage donors far more than statistics and pie charts.

Notice that something important is happening to the African charities receiving these contributed dollars. Though they work in remote, poor, and often dangerous areas, they are under intense pressure to deliver the promised work and to report promptly. There is no large organizational bureaucracy to mask project managers receiving funds. The accountability is inescapable, especially when all your donors know your e-mail address.

Democracy strikes again: with public involvement comes public scrutiny. The technology revolution in "donor" countries is adding pressure that will have a Darwinian effect in "recipient" countries: effective African organizations will prosper, ineffective ones will wither. The tough love of the marketplace is starting to have an impact.

This is no small point, especially to American donors. Direct Change stresses that bypassing major American charities in favor of "giving direct" helps "build local infrastructure" and is a major benefit of giving through their organization.

Could this "democracy" get out of hand?

I asked Ken if the rise of geographically diverse donors will lead to virtual chapters or even spin-off organizations. He replied that Direct Change has no plans for such developments, but admits "I'd love to see informal 'meet-up'-type events."

He will probably get his wish—and more. When a group of motivated individuals begins to realize its potential for affecting change, nothing stands in the way of all kinds of grassroots activity, both online and off.

Expect to see donors and activists, gathered initially online, find each other in their local communities to raise money, buy ads, hold events, and write to editors on behalf of their cause. Depending on the issue involved, local action may include confronting businesses or politicians to press for "correct" positions.

This trend is understandably both exciting and frightening for nonprofit organizations and their boards. "You have to turn over much of your branding to your donors," Ken observes. "Many traditional organizations can't do this. It's too big a cultural change."

I forecast that two trends will emerge from grassroots "virtual ownership" of the philanthropic process:

First, we will see the rise of new charities like Direct Change whose "brand" will be determined online and in communities, not in boardrooms. They will have the benefit of being nimble and flexible in their work, responding swiftly to major developments and public opinion. They will face the risk, however, of losing focus or stability, possibly splintering or being diverted from their original purpose.

Second, we will see larger, traditional charities responding by creating subbrands or spin-off subcharities that mimic Direct Change, in much the same way high-end hotel chains were forced to develop "no-frill" economy brands to remain competitive.

Some donors will be drawn to the less rigid, participatory nature of the new charities. Others will doubtlessly prefer to stick with traditional charity brands and use new technology tools to support, not to challenge, established nonprofit organizations.

What seems clear, though, is that a new category of technology-enabled charity is emerging to both strengthen and complicate philanthropy.

The competition is half-way around the world—and right down the street.

If you're a traditional charity, right about now you're thinking, "That's just great—we not only have to compete with the World Wildlife Fund and CARE. Now we have to compete with a Sudanese clinic."

Yes, you do. Not to mention a determined North Carolina teacher who needed some books for her classroom.

I'd like you to meet Amy Beckelheimer, kindergarten teacher at Raleigh's North Ridge Elementary School. She is an energetic second-year teacher—and one of thousands of educators who now routinely tap Internet tools to fund their classroom needs. Hey, I'm a sucker for an old-fashioned bake sale, but these teachers are showing just how profoundly technology is changing charity.

"I'd rather have parents give me books for my classroom than a coffee mug for Christmas."
—Amy Beckelheimer
North Ridge Elementary School in Raleigh, North Carolina

Amy wanted some *Big Books* that would help her kids learn about the world beyond North Carolina. But the set she needed cost more than $700, far more than her school's budget could afford. The PTA gives minigrants, but this was too rich for them. The idea of applying to a formal funding source wasn't on the table; what teacher has the time or experience? Besides, hundreds of teachers must be in the same boat.

Actually, thousands are. Amy heard about a new Internet-based organization called DonorsChoose.org, where teachers propose specific needs, and Web site visitors pick what they like and give what they can.

"It was so easy and painless—you just follow the steps online and write your proposal," Amy said when we spoke. "I went to Donors-Choose.org and saw hundreds of other teacher proposals and set my mind to try it." DonorsChoose sends an automated e-mail to the principal to confirm the teacher's position and the school's approval.

Within hours, Amy's proposal appeared at a site where the motto is "Teachers Ask, You Choose, Students Learn."

In a few weeks, Amy was within $151.41 of her goal—and yours truly couldn't resist putting her over the top. I made my gift around 6:00 PM on a Tuesday. Then my education about DonorsChoose really began:

- I received the obligatory confirmation e-mail a few hours later, at 11:26 Tuesday evening. It detailed my gift for tax purposes and also promised feedback on the impact of my *Big Books* in Amy's classroom.

- At 9:41 the next morning, I received an e-mail from DonorsChoose that passed along a message from Amy that can only be described as sincere and enthusiastic. But more intriguing was this tidbit:

- That same e-mail promised me "feedback from the classroom by April 4," in about ninety days. How's that for stewardship and donor service!

By now, I felt like a Rockefeller. In fact, I almost felt guilty taking the time of a busy teacher, so I e-mailed DonorsChoose and told them they could skip the feedback—though my curiosity was piqued. Their response? Not to worry, they said, the report is part of the expectation and experience—for the class. It's an important moment for the kids (who write thank-you notes) and the teacher (who expects to be held accountable).

Thank-you notes from kindergarteners? "Actually," Amy told me when I requested an interview later, "parents will come in, and the kids will dictate their thank-you, and we'll send you a picture."

I couldn't resist asking if the process was having any impact beyond providing new supplies and field trips.

"Oh, yes," Amy said. "This process is encouraging classroom innovation. School funding has to be slow because there are so many needs and so many people affected. Administrators do the best they can, but this lets teachers be very creative for their kids."

Parting advice from Amy to you: "Be positive, have confidence, and you'll get what you need." My only advice to Amy and friends: Please don't get rid of bake sales completely—we love those brownies.

Did I pick this example because it's a heart-warming fluke? Not a chance.

Amy Beckelheimer's experience has been repeated by seventeen thousand teachers who have fully funded twenty-three thousand projects through DonorsChoose, putting an amazing $10 million in classrooms according to published reports.

Ten million dollars? We'll ask the guy who started this to be your next advisor.

A flesh-and-blood, hard copy thank-you is important.
Advice from Charles Best, founder of DonorsChoose

As a former teacher, Charles Best has a healthy respect for the complexity of school budgets and the good work of established philanthropy. Even so, he has a reality check for them based on the input of thousands of people: "Donors want to avoid the black hole of school systems or big-name charities," he told me.

Fair enough. But how can you create a new kind of charity that aggregates a huge amount of money and direct it to myriad small needs?

Here are the principles Charles laid out for us:

- **Involve the widest possible group of people proposing projects or needs.** This makes a much richer experience for donors and, frankly, tests the ingenuity of those requesting funds. So, good fund-raising starts with creative programs to meet specific needs.

- **Focus on prompt donor service, including progress reports.** Offering specific giving choices means that people expect to know just when and how their gift was used.

- **Don't underestimate the human labor required, and be prepared for success.** "We were mentioned on *Oprah*, and our Web site immediately melted down. But we got back up and learned to be better prepared. Online, things can happen fast."

Charles pointedly added the importance of thanking people "offline, with flesh-and-blood, hard copy." In the case of DonorsChoose, these are the thank-you notes from students. It makes donors part of something that could easily feel too virtual and removed.

Charles had an equally intriguing and useful perspective on what fund-raisers call "major gifts," usually defined as donations with lots of zeros that were solicited in person. "We always use them to promote more citizen philanthropy." When I asked how exactly he does that, his answer illustrated a small but growing trend that could have long-term consequences for the nonprofit sector.

"Let the students give away the money."

Students? You mean give real money to kids? How much?

"It's a lot more than $300,000 already, heading toward a half million dollars," Charles says. And who is providing all this money?

"Major donors find it very refreshing. We have donors ranging from a couple in Brooklyn to a hip-hop music mogul who gave $50,000–$75,000. We put it in a pot for what we call student grant making." Hundreds of students have participated so far, going to DonorsChoose.org to allocate major gift proceeds to teachers' projects.

Charles and his donors were struck by how seriously the students took the assignment, devoting hours to studying hundreds of classroom proposals and often making selections that surprised the older generation for their insight. The Brooklyn major donor couple, Charles told me, reported to DonorsChoose that after years of philanthropic involvement, they believed "the students made wiser decisions than the professionals."

This fits into a nascent youth philanthropy movement in the United States, reflected in university student philanthropy councils at places like Ohio University, Penn State, and UC Berkeley, and youth groups within scattered international aid organizations. Among the most focused and innovative are the "girls' grant-making" efforts at about a dozen women's foundations, including those in California, Michigan, and, I'm proud to say, in my own local Chester County, Pennsylvania. Of course, kids and technology are such a natural match that tech-driven nonprofit organizations will probably become the path for large numbers of young people to learn charity and philanthropy.

The message to traditional charities and foundations is unmistakable: the students are about to become the teachers when it comes to using technology for charity. And it's a good thing, because they will be responsible for the state of philanthropy in the coming years.

Even big, fancy corporations are getting in on the act.

The rapid rise of new, online charities has triggered another major trend that has so far escaped much attention but will have widespread consequences—the reshaping of corporate philanthropy. When the people with the really big bucks start to talk about technology and donations in the same breath, you know something is going on.

7

Corporate Philanthropy Will Never Be the Same

You would expect online, interactive giving to be promoted to employees and even customers by Yahoo, eBay, Google, and other high-tech companies. It's in their corporate DNA. But the adoption of tech-driven charity by conventional retailers and manufacturing companies offers a striking lesson in changes emerging in the relationship between big business and nonprofit organizations.

Are Crate & Barrel gift certificates a wake-up call?

This year Crate & Barrel will distribute one hundred thousand gift certificates worth $25 each to its customers. But if you get one, don't start picking out cool wine glasses or new kitchen stuff; it can only be spent online at DonorsChoose.org, our enterprising teacher friends we met in the last chapter.

This is more than a feel-good promotion on the part of Crate & Barrel; it signals a new approach to corporate contribution strategy. As *The Wall Street Journal* reported in early 2007, the partnership "essentially asks customers to decide how the company should allocate charitable contributions."

The same *Journal* article also reported the DonorsChoose gift certificate distribution would account for about 3.5 percent of Crate & Barrel's entire advertising and marketing budget for the year.

That's nice, but people receive hundreds of coupons in the mail and newspapers. Did customers actually use the Crate & Barrel gift certificate coupons to contribute to DonorsChoose?

In the first test, Crate & Barrel reported a coupon redemption rate that was a stunning 550 percent higher than industry standards for regular commercial "dollars-off" coupons. "Let-the-customer-decide" philanthropy is clearly serious stuff, and it's attracting businesses and donors because it is tangible—and easy.

While corporate support for charity has a long, proud tradition, new technology allows a business to go far beyond simply writing a check, donating a percent of sales, or sponsoring an event. Projects like the Crate & Barrel collaboration with DonorsChoose put thousands of individuals in direct contact with charities for a "see-for-yourself" introduction to specific ways a donation can help. Equally important for both the donor and the charity, the online gift certificate program provides feedback on the actual results of a contribution—books delivered to classrooms, students using new art supplies, and so on. Donors are satisfied, and charities have a real shot at a continuing relationship with them.

The online gift certificate movement is gaining traction among Internet-dependent companies like Yahoo, which sends charitable gift certificates to advertising customers and employees. But some really traditional corporate philanthropists are also discovering the idea.

The Wall Street Journal went on to report that Bank of America's Family Wealth Advisors unit tested sending DonorsChoose gift certificates to its clients with a face value suitable to their affluence—the coupons averaged $500. The redemption rate? Even higher than Crate & Barrel's, with one in five Bank of America high-value customers going to DonorsChoose.org and picking a project to support according to the *Journal*.

The process of allowing customers to allocate corporate charity dollars would have been utterly impractical just a few years ago. New technology and its acceptance by the public have made it possible.

Innovative nonprofits will work increasingly with the marketing departments of supportive businesses to find new ways to use technology to involve donors.

What does this mean in the big picture? Like other kinds of charity, corporate philanthropy will never be the same—more grassroots, more accountable, and more satisfying for all parties concerned.

Make room, United Way.

Technology, especially used by the new charities, has hit workplace giving as well. GlobalGiving, for example, actually has a product line that helped fuel its early growth: building workplace-giving Web sites customized for large companies. The idea is to provide an alternative that is 180 degrees opposite of United Way's local emphasis, allowing employees of international companies to give anywhere in the world.

A vivid example is Gap, where employees can donate to projects in any country. The projects, by the way, are also nominated by employees. If you want to see how it works, just visit gapincglobalgiving.com (How's that for brand partnership?). Gap will then match every dollar an employee gives, ranging from $2,500–$10,000 annually depending on job title—even matching up to $1,000 for part-time workers. Gap pays the administrative costs, so 100 percent of the employee contribution goes to projects.

The trend is picking up speed. Hewlett-Packard's seventy thousand U.S. employees can donate on its GlobalGiving customized Web site, and Ford Motor Co. is planning a GlobalGiving portal so employees and the general public can contribute.

Of course, a business doesn't have to go as far as Gap, or be as big, to support the technology revolution in charity. Let's see how one modest corporate contribution is helping an Oregon arts group experiment with ways to ignite a new wave of giving. Financial giant ING gave $5,000 to find out if people would use ATMs for giving money away instead of taking it out.

8

Convenience Is King—The Power of Making it Easy

Impulse happens.

Impulse buying, we are told, is risky. But how much giving is based on impulse? We've all experienced the sudden desire to help a good cause, and to do so right now, while captivated by a powerful story or experience.

Whether you believe people are lazy and impatient, or merely value their time and efficiency, consider for a moment a man of the cloth who decided it was time his church could make giving easier.

To one Georgia pastor, his ATMs are "Automatic Tithe Machines."

"It's more than an ATM for Jesus," Pastor Marty Baker told a reporter just before Christmas last year. "It's about erasing barriers. We're just trying to connect with the culture."

Pastor Baker was referring to a new feature at his Stevens Creek Community Church in Georgia—two very handsome "giving kiosks" near the chapel's entrance. They were developed as a home-grown experiment in making giving easy for busy congregation members, some of whom drive for miles to attend church.

Widely reported by the media for their novelty, the machines accept credit or debit cards and are rapidly gaining popularity among the congregation. One reporter, clearly unfamiliar with the hard realities of fund-raising, observed that proceeds from the giving kiosks account for "only" one-fifth of Stevens Creek church's donations.

Only? *Only*!?

The Internet has taken years to claw its way to respectability as a significant source of online donations. This new method almost immediately attracted 20 percent of all donations. That's a positively seismic event for charity.

After watching the kiosks catch on, Pastor Baker and his wife, Patty, started a company called SecureGive to sell the machines to other churches. Within a few months, their company's Web site listed more than a dozen other churches that had already signed up for the kiosks, with many more buzzing about their potential.

But would giving-kiosk technology work outside the unique setting of a house of worship?

Let's ask the Oregon Ballet Theatre. They tried.

Give while you're "still glowing."
Advice from Jon Ulsh and Eric Jones of the Oregon Ballet Theatre

"It wasn't my idea," freely admitted Oregon Ballet Theatre (OBT) Executive Director Jon Ulsh during our interview. "I heard a story on NPR about a church that installed ATM-like giving kiosks. It occurred to me this could be perfect for us."

OBT's marketing director, Eric Jones, added that he saw the technology as a "low-pressure, convenient way for our patrons to donate while they're actually at a performance and still in the glow of what they've witnessed onstage."

The ballet contacted SecureGive, the company started by Pastor and Mrs. Baker. In short order, OBT shelled out $5,000 for each of two giving kiosks, with no idea whatsoever how they would be received.

Jon described the machines to me rather fondly as "sleek and modernistic looking," with the potential to bring new dollars for his ballet company. Expecting them to attract attention, he did what any enterprising nonprofit executive would do—he found a friendly local corporation to pick up the cost of the machines in exchange for putting its message on the kiosks' colorful screen savers.

Did soaring dancers lead to soaring support?

"We were absolutely pleased with the results," Jon reports. OBT brought in $5,000 in kiosk donations during *The Nutcracker's* short, fifteen-day run. An added bonus was the kind of people who gave—mostly holiday patrons who don't normally attend or support the ballet the rest of the year. New money, mostly from new donors.

With the rest of the season to use the kiosks, the OBT is understandably pleased and has every reason to expect the investment to produce revenue year-round. Jon and Eric point out that, even without corporate underwriting, the $5,000 per-kiosk purchase is a one-time cost, after which an organization can use the kiosk as often and for as long as it likes. (The only added cost to the ballet is a $50 monthly charge, and banks take a modest transaction fee, similar to fees for contributing by credit card online.)

Most fund-raisers would probably endorse the ballet's optimism. Anytime you can try a new fund-raising strategy and make back half the cost in the first fifteen days, you're onto something.

"We didn't expect a first-day homerun. We want to weave the kiosks into the fabric of ballet-goers lives," Jon says. It's an important insight worth emphasizing: technology does best when it is integrated into the continuing relationship between an organization and its supporters, and when it fits donors' lifestyles.

The OBT used the kiosks again three months later with a more traditional audience, including many current donors, and the machines continued to produce revenue at each performance.

Should your organization test giving kiosks? If you do, the Oregon Ballet Theatre has some advice:

- **Keep the experience very easy.** OBT's kiosks arrived with the option of collecting data about the donors, such as e-mail address. "We dropped that immediately," Jon says. "People found it cumbersome, and we watched them just give up." His advice? Take the donation and provide a helpful printed receipt—perhaps with an invitation to visit your Web site to become more involved.

- **Some people won't use the machine, so make sure they can give anyway.** OBT marketing guru Eric Jones was struck by how the kiosks "reinforced the overall idea of giving to the ballet." Many people looked at the kiosks, then turned around and handed $20 bills to ushers. (Those gifts were not counted in the $5,000 total reported to me.)

- **Be creative.** OBT is thinking of placing the kiosks with friendly businesses that support the ballet, and possibly even sharing the machines with other Portland cultural institutions.

The concept of sharing the kiosks, strategically speaking, is a really smart move that could do more than merely help Portland's many cultural organizations. The more people are exposed to this new way to give, the more it will be, in Jon's phrase, "weaved into their lives." After all, everyone is already in the habit of using ATMs. If people see them everywhere, they become another way to give, as routine as receiving a letter or phone call—but more convenient.

Keep your eye on Portland's cultural community and its pioneering ballet. My guess is that giving kiosks are only the beginning.

What else is easy and absolutely everywhere? Cell phones.

9

Feel Naked without Your Cell Phone? Just Wait

If the thought of losing your cell phone or BlackBerry sends you into a panic, you are personally experiencing only the tiny tip of a huge technology iceberg. Phones are not just getting cooler. In the words of Pierre deVries of University of Southern California's Annenberg Center for Communications, they are beginning "to add layers" to your world. Music, pictures, and text messages are just the beginning. The impact of phones will be as great on charity as on any other industry.

Why?

Because cell phones will very soon replace other things you carry for getting information and making transactions. You can already use your cell phone to make purchases, contribute, redeem coupons and even pay parking meters in many countries. The United States lags Europe and Asia by two to three years in adopting new mobile applications, including charity, because of the fragmented, consumer-resistant nature of American carriers. Even so, there are more cell phones in the United States than landlines (more than 240 million), owned by two out of every three people. In 2006, according to the National Center for Health Statistics, one in eight American homes no longer had a landline phone.

People are using their mobile phones to do more than make calls. Between ten and twelve billion text messages were sent each month last year, and the annual growth rate is 350 percent. Already more than 25 percent of Americans have used their cell phones to access news, weather, directions, stock prices, and other information—a number that will very shortly double.

Soon, using only your cell phone, you can leave behind your credit and debit cards, not to mention your ink-smudged newspaper—and your laptop.

The changes in mobile technology are so great that the people who actually build the portable handsets long ago stopped using the words "cell phone." Researchers at Motorola, possibly revealing their taste in pop music, speak of "the device formerly known as the cell phone." To most people, the rapidly evolving devices are simply "handhelds."

What your computer can do today, your phone will do in five years.

Will all this occur in some distant, far-fetched future that can be comfortably ignored?

No such luck. Mats Lindoff, chief technology officer at Sony Eriksson, notes the processing power of cell phones lags that of computers by only about five years. Think about that—what your computer can do today, your phone will be able to do in just five short years.

Of course it takes the marketplace—people like you and me—time to catch up with the newest technology. But the communications revolution makes one thing clear every day—a new phone (excuse me, new handheld) is among the quickest and easiest devices to adopt, especially if it is more convenient, more fun, and helps you leave other stuff behind.

The useful point for nonprofits, of course, is a trend that is clear, inexorable, and, I believe, full of promise. "The device formerly known as the cell phone" will become as important to charities as the computer and the printing press for three reasons:

- A handheld is the most "social" piece of technology you own, rooted in its birth as a phone. It is literally how you connect with people all day long.

- It is far more convenient than a computer—more liberating in an age when freedom of movement is a driving force.

- It serves virtually all demographics, regardless of age, gender, social condition, or geography. It is fast becoming the indispensable tool for us all.

Speaking of demographics, it's worth adding a point made by Lee Rainie at Pew Internet during our interview, especially if you're a charity looking to recruit younger donors: "There is a whole generation of young adults that simply leapt over the desktop phase most of us experienced." They learned to interact using their cell phones, which have always been far more important than their laptops for getting information and communicating. Whether young people see computers as an electronic ball-and-chain connecting them to schoolwork, or they simply can't afford one, they are learning what all of us will eventually learn, according to Lee: "Handhelds are becoming the communications Swiss Army knife, and people will take advantage of the computing power in their pocket."

In a hint of things to come, take a look at one group that is using mobile technology to help people combine charity while making what you might say is the ultimate long-distance call.

To pray in Jerusalem, press one. For Nazareth, press three. "We're just a one-way messenger to the Lord."

It's called POIP (Prayer Over Internet Protocol), a Tel Aviv-based company that allows customers to record prayers, just like leaving a voice mail for, well, you know Who. The prayers are then broadcast by discreet speakers at various religious sites in Israel. POIP cofounder and CEO Avshalom Neumann says the concept came to him after visiting Jerusalem's Western Wall. He watched people pray, dial a number on their cell phones, and hold the phones up so far-away friends and family could also pray.

POIP was born. A simple system was developed allowing anyone to call a toll-free number, use a credit card or prepaid phone card, and select a holy site from a "press one" menu. (The number was 1-888-HE-HEARS when I tried it.) The caller simply records a prayer for health, wealth, or the ideal spouse—the three most common prayers, in case you were wondering. The message is then faithfully broadcast from small speakers attached to webcams at the selected site.

Recognizing that his market extended well beyond the Jewish faithful, Mr. Neumann decided to make an exploratory sales swing through the American South. The result? U.S. demand is now growing, and prepaid POIP phone cards can be found in a growing number of Christian churches.

POIP's founders also applied one of the key rules of introducing a new technology: fit into people's lifestyle. So you can now also buy prepaid POIP cards at regional 7-Eleven stores, according to Christopher Rhoads who first covered the new company for the *Wall Street Journal* in 2007.

Churches pay a few dollars for the prepaid cards and often resell them at higher rates to help raise funds to support their work. It's an engaging, affordable, and easy way to meet a deep personal need.

Hanan Achsaf, POIP chairman, told the *Journal*, "It's just $5 or $10 and you get eternal life." Now that, as the marketing people say, is quite a value proposition.

What's next for these mobile technology pioneers?

A service that allows people a five-minute live webcam view of their favorite holy site for a dollar or two—sent to their handhelds, of course.

What about handhelds for groups that are, shall we say, less well-connected?

So far, a few American charities are experimenting gingerly with handhelds to build support:

- The ASPCA uses handhelds to keep in touch with supporters using text messages containing dog or cat health tips. The recipient pays "standard rates" for the weekly tips, and the ASPCA builds a database of mobile numbers. Of course, periodically you are encouraged to return to the ASPCA Web site to learn more. But a full year elapses, according to the ASPCA, before it asks its text recipients to donate.

- The Mile High (Denver) American Red Cross Chapter used text messages to acquire new donors as a way to help during Hurricane Katrina, and reported considerable success.

- Supporters of Planned Parenthood in Colorado startled elected officials with advocacy calls during a "virtual lobby day." The lawmakers received text messages, organized by zip code and assigned times, intended to create a cascade of support instead of a logjam.

- *Business Week* reported in 2007 that cash-strapped New Orleans is attempting a "text to give" effort to help pay the costs of reviving Mardi Gras.

To be a new technology guru, you'll have to learn two acronyms, but they're easy. First, there is SMS, or Short Message Service, which are text messages paid for by that dismal, familiar phrase, "Standard message rates apply." Second is PSMS, which just means "Premium" SMS, paid for when your phone carrier gets their rate and collects an additional amount (contribution) that they pass along to your charity. And to anticipate your possible question, 95 percent of all handhelds are capable of receiving text messages.

But for right now, at least, there is plenty wrong with PSMS, except as a way to learn the mobile ropes. First of all, U.S. carrier companies have yet to change the standard percent they keep on transactions they process, set at 40–50 percent. Second, the amount of a PSMS transaction is usually capped at $5 or $10 per transaction, or $100 per month; carriers apparently worry that big donations will add to skyrocketing phone bills, creating collection problems for them. These obstacles explain the limited testing we've seen in the United States thus far.

Having said that, Denver-based Mobile Accord is hopeful things will change. Tony Aiello works with the company's nonprofit clients, helping them experiment with a wide array of mobile applications—voting, sweepstakes, petitions, alerts, and, of course, donations.

"We are working with all the U.S. carriers to get them to embrace a new, nonprofit rate card and to identify a 'non-taxable' event," Tony said during our interview Are you kidding? Getting phone companies to loosen their choke hold on consumers' wallets? Tony believes there is an "extremely high likelihood" this will happen as pressure from consumers and nonprofits grows.

Meanwhile, other developments hold promise. PayPal Mobile offers a "Text to Buy" service allowing consumers to use their PayPal account instead of phone carrier to make purchases. Upon receiving a text order for a product, PayPal confirms the purchase with the mobile user through a pin number, processes payment, and arranges shipping of the product. Like downloading music and searching for map directions, mobile commerce will grow quickly as consumers become comfortable with the process. And, as we know, where commerce goes, charity soon follows.

But won't my phone get spammed?

Tony Aiello doesn't think so because "mobile space is a walled garden." While the Internet is an open source, with thousands upon thousands of servers capable of spewing spam, your phone line is 100 percent permission based. "Only messages you ask for will get through the billion-dollar barriers erected by your carrier." There is also a simple, industry-wide standard for halting any unwanted messages—just text "stop" in reply to any organization's SMS or PSMS, and you will be automatically opted out. If only e-mail blocking was so easy.

When carriers do adjust their rates to charity use of handhelds, what happens then?

"We'll finally be able to conduct impulse campaigns, telling people to text keywords the same way we now tell them to go to a URL," Tony believes. So stay tuned. Or jump in and try your hand.

The wireless industry has formed the Wireless Foundation to wrestle with rates and other issues, suggesting progress will occur at some point. Foundation Executive Director David S. Diggs told reporters in early 2007 that the industry was indeed trying to respond to charity needs without running afoul of laws and regulations that prevent companies from discussing pricing among themselves.

Industry players, not surprisingly, do not always agree on the best response to charity. Some have been known simply to contribute their "standard rates" in fund-raising emergencies. Others defend applying rates to charity text messages, pointing out that a fifteen-cent fee compares very favorably to the cost of a first-class stamp donors must use to mail their donation by check.

Perhaps the most significant challenge that may or may not be overcome is the difficulty of multitasking with other media while using your handheld. As Pew Internet pointed out to us, multitasking has emerged as Americans' preferred way to access media. But, freed from thinking of handhelds as phones, developers are increasingly nimble at meeting consumers' demands for more and more mobile function. My prediction is that they will find a way to make charity by handheld fun and fast, challenging the computer as an arena for donor activity.

Okay, so now we know that phones are turning into something totally new. But what about that other familiar medium, your mail? After all, isn't most American charity still conducted by check? Funny you should ask. I took a close look at the good old mailbox, and it turns out that predictions of the death of postal mail were entirely premature. Online technology has indeed had an impact on mail, but it may not be what you think.

10

Bonus Chapter—In Praise of That Lovable Old Mail

U.S. Postal Service data confirms what you already knew: even Aunt Sally doesn't send you nice, chatty letters anymore. According to a USPS Household Diary Study, only 4 percent of all household mail is actually between households; the other 96 percent is between households and businesses, government, and nonprofit organizations. Of course, Aunt Sally still sends greeting cards, and so do you, probably accounting for a big chunk of that remaining 4 percent.

Moreover, the study reports that about 60 percent of all mail is advertising. This is dandy, by the way, because it turns out that Americans *love* advertising, when it's relevant, interesting, fun, or useful. Keep that in mind as we pause to consider your organization's mailings.

The enduring popularity of mail is not just generational. It's true that the Great Generation of World War II and their baby boomer offspring looked forward to the "mailman" long before s/he became the politically correct, gender-neutral "letter carrier." Getting the mail is still a big deal for them—as it also is for Generation X and the Millennials.

Other industry studies reveal that 72 percent of these younger consumers read their mail, 70 percent have used mailed coupons, and a majority would prefer more direct mail rather than more e-mail.

Why on earth do people still like that pokey mail?

The question is important because mail is a universal method for generating charitable support. It can be one of the largest expense items in a nonprofit organization's fund-raising budget, and all too often, it competes with new technology for scarce budget dollars. While wrestling to understand the still-emerging cost-benefit of social networks, search, and e-mail, direct mail remains a known quantity and an essential fund-raising lifeline for most charities.

Direct mail is a calm port in a storm of electronic demands. And it's often easier than giving online.

Major e-mail providers who once sniggered about snail mail now work diligently to ensure that postal mail and online services support one another. Tech companies learned a big lesson even as e-mail took over the planet: one person's snail is another's escargot.

I believe there are at least three reasons for the staying power of postal mail:

- Countless e-mails and Web site visits have indeed led to a great many donations—made offline. Data from technology companies like Convio and from individual nonprofit organizations confirms that e-mail often boosts responses to mailings already sitting on the desk, confounding the efforts of budget offices to match every penny of revenue to a specific appeal vehicle. People may read their e-mail at work or on their handheld, but they often write checks from home; one reminds them of the need, the other is the cash register. For now, at least, this seems to be a pattern.

- For all the talk about technology making things fast, many people find that responding to a mailing is actually easier than giving online. Too often they may have to click through several Web site layers, perhaps use a forgotten password, and then complete a blank, online form that is usually impersonal and often unhelpful. On many nonprofit Web sites, the area that encourages (or grudgingly allows) the public to donate is a virtual ghetto, buried by organizational gatekeepers who have yet to learn how eager the public is to keep its charities strong. It remains to be seen whether Web sites or handhelds will be first to offer easier ways to give, but for now at least, giving by mail is often simpler and quicker.

- Even hardcore Internet users frequently admit in focus groups that they want their postal mail to continue, albeit at a somewhat reduced pace. They hastily check e-mail from work, at home, and increasingly from their handheld, using the delete button like a scythe to sweep away bushels of messages. They know they are less likely to miss something important if it comes by mail to their home.

Donors also seem to value the downright leisurely, undemanding nature of postal mail. There is sits, waiting patiently for your attention, not bonging upon arrival or getting in the way of pressing e-mails from your boss. With a convenience that long predates the iPod shuffle, you can sort your charitable mail, ponder it, return to it later, pass it to your spouse, or put it with the bills—all in a kind of ballet of good intentions in which you are both the star and the choreographer.

Does this mean charities can complacently continue to spend millions on postal mail? Not in an age that places a premium on choice, customization, and relevance.

So can we reconcile two seemingly very different media and make them work together? Definitely.

The challenge to mail is economics, not technology. And technology can actually help.

Consider the costly resources required by manufacturing tons of paper, its transportation as freight, the creation of your letter, and its delivery to your street by truck, van, or whatever, carried right to your door by someone in a snappy uniform. If you were to start from scratch to develop an efficient, twenty-first-century system for reaching people, it's unlikely you would come up with something so complex and resource dependent. True, the process is deeply rooted in tradition, familiarity, and community. But it is also a process that depends on paper mills, fleets of trucks, armies of workers, and the price of oil.

One day, mail in its present form will simply cost too much for charity. Response rates and donation size will be no match for costs which could well become crushing within a decade or two.

Do I believe mail will come to an end? Certainly not.

But I do believe that generic, massive, well-meaning but inefficient mail will come to an end. Darwin will insist.

What does this have to do with technology changing charity?

Rather a lot, actually, because the same technology that bedevils your CFO's cost-benefit analysis also contains the means to make mail more interesting and useful to your supporters—and more economically effective for you.

And here's news that will actually cheer your budget office. You probably don't even need to spend money on new technology tools to make your mail more effective; if you have an up-to-date e-mail system or use a good service provider, you already have them.

Three cheap ways to revolutionize your direct mail

In your heart, you know the truth about your organization's e-mail: most people do not sit in rapt attention and read your wonderful prose. They scan it to see what they need to know or what they need to do. If they think it's important, they will click back to your site to learn more or take action. Therein lies gold for your direct-mail program.

Your online communication program can offer a big boost to your direct-mail appeals in three ways:

- By providing useful and interesting e-mail content, donors will actually offer their e-mail addresses in the first place. You'll see why that's such a big deal in a minute.

- By tracking the online activities of your donors, you can find out what is most important to them about your organization.

- By integrating your e-mail with your direct mail, you will increase your mail results thanks to the reminder effect.

As it turns out, one accurate predictor of donors' commitment to a charity—and their likelihood of responding to an appeal in direct mail—is their willingness to provide an e-mail address. Of course, the willingness to "opt in" for a charity's e-mail is a sure sign of interest, so those who request your e-mail are self-identified enthusiasts. But the other reason that e-mail recipients respond to postal mail is that they know more about their charities' needs thanks to all that e-mail, even if they only read it occasionally.

Studies going back almost ten years have shown that when two groups of donors—identical except for their willingness to receive their charity's e-mail—are asked to name an organization's accomplishments, the e-mail recipients consistently cite more examples in more detail. E-mail recipients visit their charities' Web sites more often thanks to links provided in e-mail. Quite simply, e-mail produces more-informed donors who give generally larger contributions on average than those who do not receive e-mail.

But even many enlightened charities face an obstacle: they have small e-mail lists, sometimes representing only a fraction of their supporters. Why are lists so small when the whole world lives by e-mail? Certainly many people are reluctant to offer up their beleaguered e-mail address.

But a more fundamental reason is that many nonprofit organizations simply do not yet recognize that an e-mail address has an actual value as cold, hard cash, so collecting e-mail addresses is not a priority. Charities often know within a fraction of a cent the value of a postal address or a phone number. But the dollars-and-cents value of an e-mail address is often still a mystery. So, in effect, the value becomes "zero." It is just more information, so why pay money to add more e-mail addresses?

If you don't believe that e-mail addresses have value, try a simple test the next time you send a postal mailing: send the very same postal appeal to donors with an e-mail address and those without one. And send an e-mail reminder two or three weeks after your postal appeal. Now compare the total giving from your donors who receive your e-mail to that of the rest of your supporters. Such studies are becoming more common and easily yield a clear dollar value for an e-mail address.

Of course, this only works if you send e-mail that is interesting, relevant, and gets delivered. And that brings us to the use of e-mail to bring donors back to your site to identify their interests—information you can use to make your direct-mail and e-mail appeals more effective.

All good e-mail systems provide recipients a way to complete profiles or surveys, and also track the places on your Web site visited as a result of clicking on an e-mail link. If your e-mail, for example, asks donors to click to a Web page describing a new program for children, any good system will record every recipient who did so. You now have evidence of a group that is specifically interested in your children's programs. (If your e-mail system can't easily track recipients in this way, I have two important words of advice: start shopping.)

You can probably think of plenty of ways to use your e-mail and Web site to learn more about the interests and preferences of your donors, in effect creating groups of supporters whom you can target in a far more meaningful way. There are, as you can imagine, a few things that might stand in your way. Let's see how to fix them.

Silos that would even scare China.

Why haven't more groups taken advantage of e-mail to capture donors' interests and convey them to the direct-mail folks? There are several reasons.

First, many organizations have built high, sturdy walls separating those responsible for Internet activity from those responsible for raising the money by direct mail. The departmental "silos" are often cited as the single largest obstacle to increasing donations, online and off. They sometimes resemble what the Pentagon calls "hardened silos" of missiles, prepared to withstand any attack from Chinese missiles—or other departments.

Fortunately, charities are beginning to recognize that Web sites, e-mail, and other Internet activities should not be managed as a technology function any more than direct mail should. (Would you hire someone to manage your direct-mail fund-raising because he knows how to run a printing press or because she understands targeting and message development?) The Internet, first and foremost, is a two-way communication function and needs to be managed as such.

If a charity wants to maximize its investment in technology and increase the relevance of its direct mail in the bargain, fund-raisers, not tech gurus, need to be responsible for collecting and accessing the rich variety of data offered by an online database. Nonprofits willing to put technology decisions in the hands of their fund-raising and communications teams are beginning to see increased donations as e-mail supports direct-mail appeals, mail appeals offer an online response option, and donors can more easily select their preferred flow of communication by both media.

Old media made new

Your charity can take other steps to make sure your postal mail remains productive. Though they aren't related to online technology, their focus is just as squarely on the needs and situation of your donors.

First, try to think of your constituents based on who they are and not based merely on what they have done for you. Services that analyze the composition of your donor base have been with us for years and can offer important clues for guiding your direct-mail message and frequency. Cambridge, Massachusetts-based Target Analysis Group, acquired by Blackbaud in 2007, never seems to rest in its search for new and better ways to understand donors' behavior and intentions.

Target and other industry leaders like Akron, Ohio-based International Data Management Inc. (IDMI) have screened donor records for my clients, for example, simply to identify supporters' approximate ages. Predictably, their analysis showed that the rate at which different generations respond to mail appeals varied widely. The next step was obvious: vary the message or frequency of mail to fit the donor's generation.

Such data analysis can include direct-mail productivity by external criteria such as zip code or gender, and internal criteria such as seasonal preferences for giving, use of credit card, willingness to buy event tickets, and so on.

Analyzing donor databases is certainly nothing new to charity managers. For years, nonprofit organizations have segmented their donors by giving level, number of years as a donor, etc. The process is neither costly nor revolutionary and is quite productive. What is new is the need to go beyond a limited focus on past transactions. Now the challenge is to test strategies based on new data that paints a richer picture of donors' interests and engagement based on Web areas visited, e-mails opened, e-cards forwarded, etc.

The challenge is to reverse a process that has become somewhat mechanical: instead of targeting ever-smaller groups of people willing to respond to unchanging and aging mail appeals, it's time to develop new appeals that are more meaningful to more people.

Finally, it's well worth noting that technology-driven changes are afoot in the direct-mail industry with great promise for charities, notably digital printing. So far largely neglected because of its price, this new printing method will probably become the norm as falling costs approach those of old, offset-printing methods.

Printers increasingly are able to customize mailings entirely around a donor's interest and history. And I don't mean the monotonous repetition of a name or past donation amount; digital printing allows a completely new mail piece—message, pictures, signer, whatever—even for small numbers of donors. It means mailings need no longer be one-size-fits-all, an anachronistic approach in today's world. Retailers and a few charities have discovered that such mailings, while still costlier than traditional printing, can be far more productive. The use of digital printing will increase as costs continue to decline, as direct-mail managers learn more about the process—and as donors begin to expect more customized treatment.

In the unlikely event your printer tells you not to worry about digital printing, just remember that the biggest manufacturer of printing presses has already stopped making the familiar offset presses. Every piece of equipment they deliver is now digital.

Charities will come to see appeals the way donors see them—not as isolated direct mail, e-mail or phone initiatives, but as a flow of information offering a choice of ways to help. People will respond however it is most convenient at the moment.

11

"If I can't even keep up, how can I get ahead?" A Self-Assessment

It's time to offer my congratulations. You've finished most of this book, and I bet you already have some ideas for ways to use new technology for your favorite cause. Let's see. Here's a self-assessment designed to help you identify opportunities for your charity. And as you answer the questions, keep something in the back of your mind:

When you are planning, are you also preparing?

It's important to distinguish between planning and preparing, two functions that management consultants remind us are related but quite different. You can only plan based on what you know. That's the value of planning: it's based on experience and familiar forces. Experience, however, is all in the past. As long as the past is a good predictor of the future, you're set. But what if you're faced with factors that are new, for which your organization has no good precedent? Then you have to be prepared both to protect yourself from unexpected threats and to take advantage of unplanned opportunities.

Americans are experimenting with new tools for communicating, transacting, and taking action; they will support those organizations that let them use those tools. So we'll lean a bit more in the direction of preparing. How would you answer these questions for your organization?

The rise of social media and citizen journalism

1. **Is someone in your organization responsible for monitoring the online communities and blogs that actively discuss your issue?** This can be a management, staff, or even volunteer assignment—as long as the findings make it quickly to someone able to spread the word to your supporters (so they can join the discussion) and to your program experts (so they can offer facts and perspective).

2. **Are you providing tools to your supporters so they can easily show their support online and invite others to join them?** Do you include links from your Web site and e-mail to important blogs or social networks? Do you provide cut-and-paste "badges" or banners that your donors can add to their social network pages? Do you suggest language that supporters can add to their e-mail signature blocks to show support?

3. **Have you asked your supporters to identify their favorite online groups?** Do you know where your core supporters spend their time online, or are you guessing?

4. **Do you have a "Virtual Volunteer Committee" to monitor relevant online communities?** Is someone assigned to write or post comments to blogs, lead viral (tell-a-friend) campaigns, etc.? Do you have a small group outside the staff for trying new technology ideas?

5. **Do your organization's e-mail messages go beyond pushing out information and requesting donations?** Does your e-mail include interactive opportunities to rate information or programs, vote on issues, comment on content, tell the media, customize a profile, answer a survey, etc.? Do you regard your e-mail list as a single entity—or do you customize messages and actions based on donors' relationships with your charity and their interests?

"We used to have a fixed idea of who our customers were. That's changed."
Advice from Roberta MacCarthy, director of marketing and development, WGBH

Coming from a fundraising leader familiar with using technology, the comment was remarkable: "I don't know enough." Roberta MacCarthy explained during our interview that consumers are still experimenting with ways to use technology, so "fund-raising practices are changing." The bottom line? A good program must include experimentation and analysis. "We need much more research, and [nonprofit organizations] need to share findings freely," especially concerning the interests and habits of new kinds of supporters.

Putting everything from local lectures to classical music online has brought Boston-based WGBH attention from as far away as Asia. "Our focus isn't just local anymore," Roberta notes, "which we didn't think a lot about when we first began to use the Internet. We still have our core supporters, but now we're attracting new people that don't fit our historic profile."

"A few years ago," she continues, "we expected to be a portal to serve 'our' people, and now we want to be in many places—YouTube, iTunes, Google, the social networks." As a major content producer, WGBH was understandably reluctant to send Internet visitors to other places, "but we're not afraid to do that now." The key is establishing your site as a reliable location for stimulating content.

The Internet has "moved fund-raising from a transaction to a relationship that is genuinely two-way," Roberta observes. "Over half our members (so far) give us their e-mail addresses to hear from us. Many are signing up for event invitations and specialized content."

But all this technology-dependent service must pose a big challenge to her managers. There's no question, Roberta says: "Our managers have to be more nimble." She adds that "we now look for fund-raising managers who can use technology to build communities."

What about the cost?

WGBH research makes it clear that technology is essential to retaining members and their continued contributions: "I would say probably 5 percent of our fund-raising budget goes to what you could call R&D, testing and implementing new technology solutions." Roberta's various departments include Customer Service, which answers questions on everything from membership benefits to program schedules. "We have always hired people to respond to phone, mail, and e-mail," she says, "but we are starting to look for Customer Service staff comfortable with using blogs, Web communities, and online content management systems."

With those sage managerial thoughts in mind, let's resume your self-assessment.

The democratization of philanthropy

1. **Can your donors choose a specific area or project to support?** Can you identify areas in your annual operations that could become mini-campaigns online—complete with reports of results? Can donors divide their gifts among programs or program areas?

2. **Can your donors rate the importance of your projects to them?** Do you introduce a new program or project to donors and ask for comment?

3. **Do donors receive feedback on the impact of their gift in terms that are specific and not merely thematic or general?** Do you promise reporting or feedback to donors when you thank them? Are program or project leaders willing to answer questions online?

4. **Do you have a "Virtual Volunteer Committee" to support your fund-raising or advocacy programs?** Do you have a group that will start its own fund-raising pages for your charity? Does it have an action plan for the year or the next few months, based on your fund-raising needs? Do you let the

group pick among your priorities for activities or programs for which they would like to raise money online?

5. **Do you offer the tools for donors to raise money on your behalf—or on behalf of a specific area or program?** Do you remind donors they can create virtual events of their own to honor someone or celebrate an occasion? Do you remind them they can use eBay on your behalf, donating a percentage to you or conducting an auction on your behalf?

Making it easy

1. **Donate to your own organization through a mail appeal, and then make a gift online. Which was easier?** How could you make both methods easier, quicker, or more fun? Is there any information you require as part of donating that you could defer (e.g., until the acknowledgment process or later e-mail communication)?

2. **Can your supporters manage their own e-mail subscriptions and change their address, or does your staff have to do it for them?** Can your donors easily change the frequency, amount, or method of their contributions? Do you offer the option of renewing support automatically?

3. **Are there convenient, visible navigation links throughout your Web site for visitors to donate and sign up for e-mail?** Find out the most frequently visited pages on your site. Do these pages contain links to donate and sign up for e-mail?

4. **Have you asked donors what they find most and least convenient about donating to your charity?** Do you test alternate online giving forms to determine which is most effective for raising money or generating e-mail signups?

Every organization has its own distinctive reality and culture, and anything you do with technology has to be comfortable to be successful. But the more you test new initiatives or strategies, the more you may challenge the status quo and force your charity outside its comfort zone. So here is some wisdom from another advisor, plus five more questions I believe you will find helpful.

"We approach a new thing like it's the old thing."
Advice from Mark Fuerst, founder of the Interactive Media Association (iMA)

Mark began our interview by saying that "It's often easier for people without experience to do great things."

In a culture that values résumés and accomplishments, it was a striking statement. Mark Fuerst has a valuable perspective, given that his professional location could be described as ground zero for changes in media and communications. Mark founded the iMA specifically to provide the nation's public broadcasters a place for serious exploration and strategic response to technology changes. His iMA meetings involve nonprofits and technology companies of all sizes and interests, and are widely regarded as some of the most stimulating in the sector.

As the former head of a public radio station and advisor to many more, Mark understands the difficulty of change in the close-knit culture of a charity. "The senior managers who hold the budget dollars for new technology are often committed to old ways, to the things that produced their past successes." Often, Mark believes, it's best to place new technology budgets and decisions in the hands of people free from a dedication to the past. In scanning scores of public broadcasting organizations, whose very existence is being decided by technology, Mark observed that he could think of only one who "picked the online manager to be their Chief Operating Officer."

He emphasized that organizations wanting success in the Web 2.0 world need to have a meaningful institutional goal driving their technology efforts. "The goal of the Canadian Broadcasting Corporation, for example, was not to have a great Web site, but to be the number-one online source for news in their country. They approached their

Web site that way and measured everything they did that way." It is a very useful example that I hope provokes a productive conversation in your charity, starting with one question: How can technology help accomplish a major goal that will advance your mission?

In an observation that recalled the Pew Internet findings, Mark added, "We need to focus on the behavioral changes in the way people use media." He went on to note that "all past media have succeeded only when they fit into people's lives. People don't wake up in the morning in order to hear the news on the radio; the news is on in the morning because that's when people wake up." Does your organization give its "news" to people when and where they want it? And when and where they can act on it?

Mark closed with a reminder that adopting new communication technology is a voluntary decision and needs internal advocates: "No one is forcing us to change, so it's often a slow process." But, he reminds us, our supporters are already making the changes in their own lives. "How can any organization plan for the future without significant attention to new trends like the mobility of information?"

How indeed.

Of course, you will not be among those left behind by technology changes. And just to make sure, let's finish your self-assessment with some candid questions about your charity's situation and potential.

Your Web 2.0 assets and liabilities

1. **What are the greatest assets you have for responding to the technology revolution?** A very involved base of support? A wide variety of ways to donate to your programs? Access to good writers or photographers? A culture of testing and analysis? Project or program personnel who love to describe the impact of their work? Strong business supporters willing to help spread the word? A group—even a small one—of young donors in your database? A board member who advocates experimenting? You get the idea.

2. **What are the greatest liabilities you need to overcome?** Are communication issues absent from organizational planning? Are your various public constituencies (donors, advocates, event attendees, etc.) considered the "property" of various departments or a shared resource receiving coordinated communications?

3. **Does your organization know its technology benchmarks and "leading indicators?"** How many supporters (new and old) actually open your e-mail? How many have ever—or never—clicked back to your Web site to complete a requested task? Can you identify those who ignore your e-mail, and do you have a plan to try to motivate them to get involved? What percent of your Web site visitors register to get your e-mail? What percent of people who visit your online donation form "abandon" the form, i.e., don't complete it? Have you tested different donation forms? When someone signs up for e-mail or makes an online gift, does your thank-you e-mail take them to an activity, survey, blog, etc.—and how many go there? You can probably think of measurements that are more meaningful to you, so keep monitoring; when you know your benchmarks you will begin to find ways to improve them.

4. **Does your budgeting process allow you to respond to the most popular new social media trends?** Is your "free media" budget (e.g., public information, press relations, etc.) fully committed to traditional media, or is a percentage devoted to social media, blogs, etc.?

5. **If you are an executive or board officer, have you given permission to your organization to test new efforts—knowing some may be unproductive?** When is an unproductive test a "failure" and when is it a useful learning? Are expectations fully and candidly discussed in advance, and results equally reviewed whether good or bad? Do you apply

old standards of success to new activities, or do you allow base-line performance to be established before setting goals?

Your answers may take shape over time—but your future as a charity technology leader won't be secure without two more valuable viewpoints. Your next advisor has plenty of experience, plus the data to go with it. Meet Jeff Regen, vice president of online marketing and communications for Defenders of Wildlife.

"Blogs and social networks are the new free media." *Advice from Jeff Regen, Defenders of Wildlife*

Jeff offered to tackle the biggest question first during our interview: Does using new technology increase overall giving? His answer was emphatic: "There's no doubt that online is growing the pie. It's a quantum transformation." Citing his extensive analysis at Defenders of Wildlife and twenty other major groups for which he has studied data, Jeff said, "Online, we're reaching people not reached effectively by other media, and they are able and willing to help."

He also noted that the combination of lower costs and bigger gifts online produces a dramatically higher net revenue for Defenders' far-flung wildlife programs. Although online donors currently represent less than 10 percent of all gross revenue, they represent closer to 15 percent of all net revenue. But new donors giving a per capita boost to the bottom line are only part of the story.

"Online donors are about fifteen years younger than direct mail donors—and online advocates (who sign petitions and forward messages) are about twenty years younger." In other words, Defenders of Wildlife is actively recruiting its next generation of donors, and Web 2.0 media play a central role.

"Nonprofits thrive on enthusiasm. That's why social networking, blogs, and other online gathering places have such huge potential," Jeff points out.

For quick, measurable growth, Defenders of Wildlife uses our friends at Care2 for recruiting activists. In terms of spending, Jeff notes, Care2 is now "our largest marketing partner."

But it doesn't always require money. It is equally useful to think of blogs and social networks, he says, as unpaid media—but with more credibility than press releases. "They take time and thought, but the cost is trivial compared to direct mail, telephone marketing, broadcast, or print advertising."

It's worth adding that Defenders of Wildlife does not approach the still-unfolding world of social networking with wide-eyed optimism, but with long-term, strategic goals. "Do we make any money from social networks? Not yet." So why does the organization put in the time when it is already so busy? Jeff cited three reasons, which succinctly bridge the gap between planning and preparing:

"First, we do it to learn. It's very hard to enter a new activity years after it's matured and you're playing catch-up.

"Second, and more important, we want to be a creator, not an observer, of social networks and how they work.

"Third, we have a mission that depends on public support. Why are we experimenting with social networking? Because we want to affect public opinion."

That, as the saying goes, is keeping your eye on the ball.

When investing time and money, "Take the long view." *Advice from Vinay Bhagat, founder and chairman of Convio*

Vinay has certainly taken his own advice, accepting the need for his technology company to test, retest, and evolve, accepting the verdict of the donor marketplace and focusing on two principles: First, give supporters the easiest, most interesting tools possible. Second, relentlessly analyze the results to learn what strategies and practices are the most effective.

Why is Web 2.0 such a big deal?

"Donors are demanding more control of their giving," Vinay says, "whether it's skipping a monthly payment, splitting a donation between two projects, or picking the format of the reports they receive." Groups that are the most successful online are providing exactly those tools.

Vinay also confirms an irreversible trend, based on the experience of Convio: online services that donors can customize for themselves were once merely desirable but are swiftly becoming essential.

What's more, it is difficult, if not impossible, for a charity to attempt to create the required array of tools itself, or by stitching together a virtual quilt of hit-and-miss solutions. "Build-or-buy is an outdated decision-making model," he says. Notwithstanding his perspective as a technology provider, the evidence across the sector supports his view. The largest charities do not outsource technology solutions because they are rolling in cash and can afford it; on the contrary, they do it because even they *cannot* afford to do it themselves. The same is no less true for charities of modest means. The need to keep up with the public's demand for security, customization, ease, speed, and reliability is far beyond any charitable group's means, and indeed beyond its competency or mission.

The Web, e-mail, search, and many other online features may be free, but the technology required to use them effectively is not. So we're talking about a more realistic look at the cost of doing business in the twenty-first century?

Yes, Vinay says, pointing out that "organizations know how to take the long view of an investment. They did it with direct mail originally," and still do, accepting short-term losses to further long-term financial security. Emphasizing his point, he reminds us that a serious commitment to technology is an organizational commitment, starting at the top. The groups that are most successful with online technology are "those that have a strong, high-level advocate for change, including advocates on the board," he adds.

I noted that many charities are familiar with basic online tools but are sometimes unsure where to go next. He replied that "the [nonprofit] sector has moved from early adoption to acting as a much broader laboratory." Organizations are discovering that success isn't so much about best practices, but is based on a higher level of education about how people are using technology. One of the biggest challenges to the sector is "the need for much greater know-how and institutional capacity" to understand and respond to the power and demands of technology. "Constituents," he adds, "are leading nonprofits into technology," and are attaching themselves to groups that understand their preferences.

Certainly your charity wants to succeed—and it has to survive—in this changed and changing world. The difference between success and survival lies in making choices that are worth weighing before we part company.

12

Survival or Success—It's Time to Pick One

Because commercial markets are often swift and always unforgiving, an ineffective business can be drastically reduced or even wiped out in a short time span. But, employees' and stockholders' pain notwithstanding, the consumer is usually the winner. In the famous phrase of economist Joseph Schumpeter, intense competition breeds "creative destruction." General Motors, for example, might decline or vanish while consumers flock to other companies making better cars. GM loses, consumers win.

Charity is, of course, a different kind of market, apt to change much more slowly as loyal individuals try to keep a struggling organization afloat rather than respond to the needs of a wider market. Nevertheless, technology is accelerating the process by which nonprofit organizations will ultimately face "creative destruction."

There is nothing new about this. Charities have prospered or faltered since the very beginning. I simply don't want your organization to be on the list of casualties as new technology changes charity.

The management experts tell us the strategies for survival can be very different from those for success. Why? Essentially because survival is defensive and focuses from the inside out, driven more by limitations than opportunities. A strategy for being wildly successful, on the other hand, has an outside-in focus, driven by seizing opportunities.

In the case of Web 2.0, a strategy to survive has real risks. I've seen evidence that an overcautious strategy means dipping a toe in technology in a way that is isolated from a charity's mainstream communications. This strategy is likely to lead to underinvestment (either in money, attention, or patience), and therefore to testing efforts that are fated to fail. A series of hesitant, unrelated, or isolated tests not only fails to yield enough experience on which to build, but produces false conclusions: "We started a blog and hardly anyone posted comments, so blogs don't work for us."

Deciding to succeed, on the other hand, means developing an organization-wide goal of using technology to provide something important, exciting, and useful to the community. It means beginning to shift your resources and your thinking to meeting donors' growing need for participation, self-expression, and convenience.

You can see where all this has taken us: embracing Web 2.0 tools to attract greater support is not fundamentally a technology decision but an organizational one.

Do more choices mean more giving?

No one knows the answer to one of the biggest questions posed by the technology revolution: whether charity will grow in America. Public contributions have always had slight ups and downs, but have hovered pretty steadily a bit above 2 percent of the gross domestic product for many years. If you believe giving is mostly a product of tax policy, or a carefully considered act based on people's general idea of their charitable budget, then significant growth is probably unlikely. Certainly there are many who *do* have a charitable budget, and their giving may or may not be affected by an explosion of new ways to give and new charities.

But there are millions of Americans with strong feelings about their causes and who, I believe, are open to doing more. The technology revolution is producing evidence that charity has been trapped for decades by communication methods that too often segregate the act of giving from everyday life. The act of donating to a good cause may be called charity, but the process has been captured by the word "fund-raising," which reduces a glorious experience to an ask-and-answer, push-pull process: nonprofits ask for help (endlessly, as many donors say), and generous individuals are faced with mounting requests to which they must reply yes or, increasingly, no.

It's no wonder that the participatory, peer-driven, borderless charity experience provided by new technology is gaining popularity, despite its casual and unfamiliar elements.

I believe that new online and mobile tools, because of their availability, interactivity, and human connectivity, will finally allow charity to compete with consumer spending. Certainly no one will struggle deciding whether to buy groceries or make a donation. But a great amount of spending by Americans, by their own admission, is often wasteful, unnecessary, or impulsive. I believe Dennis Whittle is on to something important when he says that GlobalGiving is tackling consumer spending head-on, and I believe charity will increase as a result of the forces behind Web 2.0 and future Webs yet unnumbered.

"We didn't create all this technology to isolate people."

Debra May Hughes is president of Public Interactive, which provides content to public broadcasting stations, and her words struck me as a great reminder of the spirit of Web 2.0. "We [technology developers] never imagined people in isolation, huddled over their computers," she told a conference in 2007. New technology, she says, is about getting involved, connecting with others, and being part of the action. It is definitely not about being a bystander.

You've been introduced to many good organizational role models in these chapters. They vary in mission and size, but their approach to technology is strikingly similar: involve donors in helping raise awareness and funds, aggressively seek new supporters, test a wide variety of new technologies, use external partners to reach new constituents, and commit to the process of learning the ways of Web 2.0.

I believe all the virtual advisors you've met here would agree with technology leaders who like to say, "The Internet finally belongs to you." I would only add, "Make the most of it for your cause."

Acknowledgments

Writers customarily thank their families, and now I know why. An astonishing number of hours are claimed by a book, even one as modest as this. So I want to thank my wife, Heidi, for her support through all four seasons and for her confidence and probing questions. Also my thanks go to three great kids, Daniel, Ellie, and Ted, for their patience and interest.

I thank my colleagues at McPherson Associates, beginning with Lisa Marie Daniels whose insights and observations strengthened the book's concepts and final manuscript. Thanks also to Liz Flood, Tim Oleary, and Rebecca Jackson for their input and encouragement. And I owe a great deal to Andrew Levison, a friend who helped me appreciate just how much technology is about people, and who has been my tech sherpa for many years.

My thanks go across the Atlantic to a good friend and business conspirator, Bernard Ross, for his counsel and irreverent wisdom. Many thanks are also due to Ken Burnett for his generous advice and encouragement.

It would be ungrateful indeed if I failed to acknowledge my clients, whose interest in new technology constantly stimulates my thinking and helps me appreciate how much is as stake. They do the hard work of putting ideas into practice, and I am proud to be their colleague.

For several years, I have had the privilege to teach technology trends at New York University's George H. Heyman Jr. Center for Philanthropy and Fundraising, and I want to thank the center's chairman, Naomi Levine, and Director Lewis Brindle, for supporting for my ever-evolving course.

I also want to acknowledge the editorial staff at iUniverse for their encouragement and patient, thorough review of my manuscript, and the Editorial Board for designating my book as an "Editor's Choice" selection.

Finally, my deepest thanks go to the individuals interviewed for *Digital Giving,* named prominently in the chapters both as an expression of appreciation and to help you remember their names so you can thank them yourself one day. On the following pages are the URLs for their Web sites. Probably the richest educational experience you can have on this topic is to visit each site, subscribe to its e-mail, contribute, or join, and then watch carefully. The process will continue to provide you with advice, ideas, and inspiration. And if any of the people you read about here ever ask for *your* advice, please give it as generously as they have.

Indispensable Resources

Web sites

www.aspca.org
www.care2.com
www.convio.com
www.defenders.org
http://directchange.org
www.donorschoose.org
www.gather.com
www.globalgiving.com
www.google.com and http://labs.google.com
www.idmi.com
www.integratedmedia.org
www.kshs.org
www.mcphersonassociates.com
www.mobileaccord.com
www.momsrising.org
www.obt.org
www.pewinternet.org
www.po-ip.com
www.targetanalysis.com
www.unfoundation.org and www.nothingbutnets.net
www.wgbh.org
www.wikipedia.org

Books

Anderson, Chris. *The Long Tail.* New York: Hyperion, 2006.

Gillmor, Dan. *We the Media: Grassroots Journalism by the People, for the People.* Sebastopol, CA: O'Reilly Media, 2006.

McConnell, Ben and Jackie Huba. *Citizen Marketers: When People are the Message.* Chicago: Kaplan, 2007.

Surowiecki, James. *The Wisdom of Crowds.* New York: Doubleday, 2004.

Tapscott, Don and Anthony D. Williams. *Wikinomics: How Mass Collaboration Changes Everything.* New York: Penguin, 2006.

About the Author

Richard C. McPherson

Richard McPherson created national advocacy and fundraising campaigns on behalf of civil rights and conservation causes before founding McPherson Associates in 1984. He has advised Mrs. Martin Luther King, Jr., former President Jimmy Carter, the United Nations Environment for Europe Program and leading nonprofit organizations in the U.S. and Europe. He consults with causes that include conservation, women's rights, higher education, the arts and public broadcasting, and is a faculty member of New York University's George H. Heyman Jr. Center for Philanthropy and Fundraising. McPherson Associates, Inc., is based near Philadelphia and is the Online Communications partner for The Management Centre in London. He can be reached at digitalgiving@mcphersonassociates.com.

Cover Design

Ben 2.0 was created for *Digital Giving* by Joe Warner and his talented team at 20/10 Design and Marketing. It captures the spirit of the book by shifting the familiar image of Benjamin Franklin from U.S. currency to a circuit board.